LET ME STAND AT YOUR SIDE

LET ME STAND AT YOUR SIDE

M. BASILEA SCHLINK

Evangelical Sisterhood of Mary
Darmstadt-Eberstadt, West Germany

© Evangelical Sisterhood of Mary, 1975

ISBN 3 87209 614 1

Original Title:
Ich will hier bei Dir stehen — Jesu Lieben und Leiden damals und heute
First German Edition — 1975
First English Edition — 1975
Second Printing — 1977

The verses from *Evangelisches Kirchengesangbuch* (EKG) have been used by kind permission of the Kirchenverwaltung der Evangelischen Kirche in Hessen und Nassau, Darmstadt.

Bible quotations are taken from the Revised Standard Version of the Bible, copyrighted 1946 and 1952 by the Division of Christian Education of the National Council of the Churches of Christ in the U.S.A., and used by permission.

Cover Photo: The Lamb of God, from the Isenheim Altar by Matthias Grünewald (1460 to 1528), with kind permission of the Société Schongauer (Musée d'Unterlinden, Colmar, France).

Printed in **West Germany**

TABLE OF CONTENTS

THE PASSION SERVICE

PREFACE

The most precious treasure, as many devout men of God have testified in word and song, is the suffering of Jesus for our redemption. Over the course of the years a longing grew in my heart — it was my fervent prayer to be able to accompany Jesus more closely along His path of sorrows. And the Lord answered this plea.

Years later I had the privilege of spending some time at the sites of His sufferings in the Holy Land and upon my return I felt compelled to write something for my spiritual daughters about the sufferings of Jesus. A diary entry of mine in Lent 1960 reads, "Grant me something for my daughters so that every Maundy Thursday and Good Friday they can truly accompany You in spirit along Your path of suffering. Help me to give a vivid representation so that their love for You may be set aflame."

Shortly afterwards, during a special week in Lent, the Lord granted me the fulfilment of this request. Moved by His Spirit, I spoke on tape about Jesus' entire path of suffering, and the recording, which lasted many hours, was interspersed with songs and prayers. This text then helped us to accompany Jesus prayerfully along His way of the cross every year during the night of Maundy Thursday and on Good Friday. Through this experience my daughters' relationship to Jesus in His sufferings was deepened from year to year and their joy grew as they encountered the overwhelming love of Jesus revealed in His sufferings for us. Guests who have celebrated Easter with us have asked how it is possible to receive the tremendous joy of Easter that they could sense here on our little Land of Canaan. And when they heard of our Passion Service, they too yearned to take part in it.

Over ten years have since elapsed and the sufferings of Jesus today have assumed untold proportions. Therefore, should not this service be held at other places too, and not only on the little Land of Canaan? Should not those who love Jesus have the opportunity to gather together here and there, in their homes, to watch with Him on the night of His sufferings, united in the prayer, "Let me accompany You with my love"? In this day and age should not Maundy Thursday and Good Friday be characterized everywhere by a spirit of love and thanksgiving, dedication to bear the cross, adoration and rejoicing at such a redemption? Is there not all the more reason for this *today* in view of Jesus' present-day sufferings? His degradation in numerous publications, in stage and film productions is a challenge to us to prepare to suffer for Him out of love when perhaps very soon suffering will strike us as the members of His Body.

Down through the ages the children of Israel have observed the night of their deliverance, the night when the Lord brought them up out of Egypt. No Jew is permitted to forget the night when the Lord delivered them after four hundred years in bondage, the night when a lamb was symbolically slain in each house and the doorposts and lintel were sprinkled with its blood. Should we not, therefore, observe the night of our redemption — an eternal redemption from all the torment of sin, death and hell?

The passages marked by asterisks are like pictures of Bible stories, intended to convey a more vivid representation of the sufferings of Jesus. They are summaries of portions of *Das bittere Leiden unseres Herrn Jesu Christi* (The bitter suffering of our Lord Jesus Christ) by Clemens Brentano, a famous German writer. His book is based on the accounts of Anna Katharina Emmerich, a woman of prayer, who described to him what the Lord had inwardly revealed to her in prayer about His sufferings.

A tape recording, lasting about six hours, has been made of this service. A set of five tapes recorded at 3³/₄ ips. on 5″ reels (or cassettes), is available for purchase or loan. Please write to
The Evangelical Sisterhood of Mary
P.O.B. 13 01 29, D-6100 Darmstadt 13
West Germany

OPENING

all sing

> Lamb of God, pure and sinless,
> Upon the cruel tree martyred,
> Ever meek, ever patient,
> Although despised and slandered!
> Hadst Thou not borne all wickedness,
> Despair would overcome us.
> Have mercy on us, O Jesus.

cf. EKG 55
(Evangelisches Kirchengesangbuch)

opening prayer

all sing

> Holy week of holy suff'ring —
> God's Son goeth forth to die.
> Step by step I would go with Thee,
> Ever staying at Thy side.

> For today anew, my Saviour,
> Thou must tread this path of woe.
> Scourging, thorns, disgrace and slander
> Once more greet Thee here below.

> Yet in all Thy bitter suff'ring
> Thou shalt not remain alone.
> May this week to me be holy;
> Make Thy sorrows now my own.

> Jesus, we would watch beside Thee,
> Always Thee with love surround.
> We would comfort and console Thee,
> To Thy love with love respond.

Week of suff'ring, days so holy,
Pathway of the Lamb Divine!
May'st Thou find us loving, watching,
Mindful of each plea of Thine.

melody WJ 48 [1] or
"Jesus Calls Us o'er the Tumult"

all speak

Jesus, Jesus, my Belovèd,
Lamb of God, now glorified,
Once You chose the cross of suff'ring,
Willingly for us You died.
Let me, Lord, with love now follow
On Your path of pain and death;
Let me feel the grief and anguish,
Which You felt at ev'ry step.

choir

Jesus, Jesus, my Belovèd,
How I worship and adore
Such great love, such bitter suff'ring
That You in Your Passion bore!
Let me trace Your holy footsteps
Where You wept in agony.
Let me now my whole life offer,
For You bore such pain for me.

[1] WJ stands for *Well-spring of Joy,* songs of the Sisters of Mary

11

JESUS ON THE WAY TO GETHSEMANE

My Saviour goes to suffer,
Belovèd Lamb of God.
O let me stay close by You
And share Your way, dear Lord.
Because of me You suffered
And for my sake You died.
Let me lament my sinning
And stay close by Your side.
O let me now go with You,
My dearest Lord and King;
Filled with contrition join You
In Your night of suffering.

On Maundy Thursday evening Jesus set out from Mount Zion, where He had celebrated the Last Supper with His disciples in the Upper Room. His soul was in deep anguish. Judas had left to betray Him.

Jesus departed from the city most likely via the western gate. Then He descended the hill and crossed the Kidron Valley in order to reach the Garden of Gethsemane. Altogether it was about half-an-hour's walk.

Unlike the three previous years, Jesus was no longer accompanied by *twelve* disciples as He walked along this path. Satan had taken possession of one of them. Thus Jesus had only eleven disciples with Him as He went down into the Valley of Kidron, the Valley of Jehoshaphat. Judas was on his way to arrange the betrayal, while Jesus was making His way to Gethsemane, to the garden of the oil press. There God Himself intended to tread His Son as in an oil press.

As it is written, Jesus went before His disciples on the path to Gethsemane. The disciples followed single file because of the narrowness of the paths leading down into the Kidron Valley. On the way Jesus held an important conversation with them before entering the garden.

Jesus is truly the Good Shepherd, who in His great love sees the danger threatening His sheep. This is why He warns them beforehand, why He seeks to help them and prepare them. He does not take them into the Garden of Gethsemane without speaking once more of the dreadful events that would soon begin, so that they might prepare themselves.

He says to them, "You will all fall away because of me this night; for it is written, 'I will strike the shepherd, and the sheep of the flock will be scattered'" (Matthew 26:31).

How Jesus yearned to prepare His disciples! And not only now before the battle in Gethsemane begins. No, of late Jesus had sought time and time again to impress upon His disciples the gravity of the impending hour. He had said to them, "You know that the Passover will take place the day after tomorrow. Then the Son of man will be handed over to be crucified." Could anyone be more explicit than when he names a specific date — in two days' time such-and-such a terrible event will occur?

When Mary of Bethany anointed Jesus, He said, "She has anointed My body beforehand for burying." With that Jesus openly stated that in a few days' time He would be buried. Moreover, at the Last Supper the disciples personally heard the Lord say that one of them would betray Him. They knew that during the past few days the Pharisees had frequently met for consultation with the intent to kill Jesus. The atmosphere was ominous. Even if Jesus had not spoken to them of the dreadful suffering that awaited Him, they should have sensed it.

But Jesus' words seemed to hit an iron shield. The disciples did not want to know anything about the cross. The thought of suffering was intolerable to them. They refused to enter suffering with Jesus. With their ears they heard Jesus say that the cross und suffering awaited Him — and if it struck Him, it would strike them too — but they closed their hearts to the idea of suffering. They repressed the thought of the coming affliction, because such a path seemed too hard to them. But that meant that they did not want to accompany Jesus along His path of sorrows. And indeed, none of them could be found at His side when He trod the bitter path of the cross along the Via Dolorosa.

In those last days it must have been immeasurably hard for our Lord Jesus to be in such close company with His disciples, who had always been at His side wherever He went during the three years of His public ministry. Jesus' heart was filled with suffering. He lived wholly in that which awaited Him and which constantly confronted His soul — His path of bitter suffering that would lead to death. He yearned to speak with His disciples about the coming suffering in His tender care for them, but also in His love, for love longs to share everything — especially sorrow — with the beloved. However, Jesus found no loving response, no understanding. He found no one to suffer with Him. Forsaken by all, Jesus had to begin His hard path of affliction alone.

How strong the disciples' resistance to suffering was, was revealed by their reaction. Before entering the Garden of Gethsemane, Jesus once more clearly told them what would befall Him. At these words it would have been only natural for them to turn to Him and beseech

Him, "Lord, equip us with strength, that we may be able to endure." But no, they remained silent.

The disciples, though no doubt full of fear, were sure of themselves. Deep down inside they knew that one must consecrate oneself to the cross with a "Yes, Father" and that this act of dedication must be made in advance, because otherwise one would be taken unawares by the enemy in the hour of affliction and defeated. But they did not act accordingly. They were unwilling to face up to the fact that without making a dedication to suffering, without consenting to the cross, one cannot be steadfast in the hour of trial.

In contrast to this self-assurance of the disciples, Jesus was filled with trepidation, as He expressed to them, "My soul is exceedingly sorrowful, even unto death." The disciples remained self-confident, because they did not want to accept the fact that suffering and the cross awaited Jesus — and them also. This is what made Peter vow shortly before they went to Gethsemane, "I will go with You even if I have to die." Ultimately they repressed the thought that Jesus' work could soon lie in ruins. They could not bear to think of Him standing powerless in the sight of all men — yes, being led off like a criminal and condemned to death.

But Jesus, the Creator of all worlds, did not live in this self-assurance; He was filled with fear at the thought of the suffering. Earlier, when He had spoken of the baptism of suffering that awaited Him, He said, "How great is My distress till it is over!" Thus Jesus prepared to meet suffering by surrendering His will to the Father, whereas we, who are mere created beings and sinners, suppress the possibility or fact that suffering could enter our lives in our false self-confidence. This we do when we reject the cross.

The distance that separated the disciples from Jesus

was immeasurable, although outwardly they were at His side. Jesus wanted the cross and suffering, and He gave His consent. But the disciples refused the cross; their answer was a NO. Jesus submitted to the will of God; they rebelled against it.

Jesus entered the Garden of Gethsemane with His disciples, deeply sorrowful, also grieving over them. It was His last attempt to reach them, but His words had fallen on deaf ears.

Before we enter the Garden of Gethsemane in spirit with Jesus in this holy night of His suffering, let us remember the bitter disappointment the disciples inflicted upon our Lord in the hour of Gethsemane, and pray:

all pray

Forgive us, Lord Jesus, when like Your disciples long ago we do not want to hear anything about the suffering that will enter our lives, although You wish to prepare us for it. Forgive us, for in doing so we forsake You. So often we do not accompany You along the way of the cross, when You call us to do so. Break our iron-like resistance to suffering, the shield that we raise time and again to protect ourselves. This we pray, trusting that You will bring us through and that in Your love You will not lay more upon us than we can bear.

Let us not grieve You, dear Lord Jesus, by our unwillingness to bear the cross, for how grieved You must be to see so few of Your own accompanying You along the way of the cross, especially in Your suffering today.

Amen.

JESUS IN THE GARDEN OF GETHSEMANE

choir

O Jesus, lonely while men sleep,
For none with You their watch will keep.
You are alone, forsaken;
This lonely path You've taken.

You knock, You plead and You implore;
Your friends go with You now no more.
You are alone, forsaken;
This lonely path You've taken.

WJ 51

An inexpressible sadness filled our Lord Jesus that night in the Garden of Gethsemane. Indeed, He could already sense fear and temptation approaching Him menacingly from all sides. For this reason He bade His three disciples, "Remain here, and watch with Me."

What love and humility are expressed in this request of Jesus, who asks His pitiful disciples to stay by Him, although they would later disappoint Him so deeply. We know that Jesus is also asking us to remain with Him when His heart today is filled with anguish because His own are falling away and mankind is sinking in sin and blasphemy. Thus our fervent plea is, "Lord, help us, Your disciples of today. You know how pitiful we are too. Help us to truly partake of the suffering that You are now enduring."

In that night in the Garden of Gethsemane Jesus withdrew into a cave. Horror and dread came over Him and He began to shake and tremble. The powers of darkness assailed Him so violently that He was cast to the ground. The horrors were too great for Jesus to let the disciples witness and for this reason He had withdrawn a stone's throw away from them.

The forces of hell, Satan and his hordes, now began to draw close. They pressed in on Jesus, who in this hour, probably more than ever before, had returned His divinity to the Father. Jesus, who had taken upon Himself full humanity, lay stretched out on the ground, as Matthew writes, and was almost tormented to death by these powers.

choir

> Gethsemane! Who hears His pleading,
> His woeful crying and entreating?
> The Son of God in anguished fear
> With none to solace Him is here.
> He is alone, forsaken.
>
> Gethsemane! Who notes His yearning,
> Who sees Him to His friends now turning,
> That He may His deep grief impart,
> And they may cheer, console His heart?
> Alas! His friends are sleeping.
>
> Gethsemane! Who sees Him wrestling,
> With evil pow'rs around Him pressing,
> Tormenting Him with all their might?
> And in His soul He sees no light,
> By God and man forsaken!

WJ 53

The words that Jesus had spoken to His disciples shortly before entering Gethsemane now came true. He had told them that God would strike Him, the Shepherd. Gethsemane means oil press. There God Himself trod the most precious fruit of mankind, the Son of man and the Son of God. God struck His only Son, whom He dearly loved, with blow upon blow, so that the most wonderful drink of all would be pressed out for mankind. The Father's heart must have wept and lamented to inflict such blows upon His only-begotten Son, the essence of purity and divine graciousness.

What cries of lamentation must have filled the heavens in this hour! Lamentations of the angels, the Father and the Holy Spirit. No human heart could ever comprehend this. The Father had to conceal Himself from His beloved Son. Out of love for us He had to harden His heart towards Jesus. The Son was forsaken in His abysmal suffering, tormented by the hordes of hell, and God was far away. He gave no answer to His Son.

choir

> Unanswered His plea,
> Forsaken is He,
> To powers of darkness abandoned.
> The heart of the Father seems hardened.
>
> With anguish untold
> God's heart must behold
> The soul of His Son in such torment.
> Yet He must remain now so distant.

In this hour when He was completely forsaken by the Father as well as by His disciples, the true nature of Jesus, the Son of God, was revealed — heart-moving childlikeness, deep humility, supreme nobility and loving dedication to suffering.

In the midst of severest temptations, when the hordes

19

of hell closed in on Jesus and tormented Him, He proved Himself to be a Child of the Father, full of trusting love, submerging His will in the will of the Father. That which truly fills our hearts is revealed when we are in suffering. Jesus' heart was pure love. Nothing but love flowed forth from Him — love for the Father and for the sons of men, whom He had created. Even now when the Son could truly no longer understand the Father and when a feeling of defiance could have arisen in Him against the Father, His heart overflowed with pure love towards His Father in heaven. And towards His disciples Jesus exhibited a love that could not be disappointed, a love that sought them out ever anew, a love that continued to love them to the very end despite their disgraceful behaviour.

No one but our Lord Jesus could show such love in deep suffering. And whoever has not yet really known or loved Jesus must love and worship Him for this.

Come, let us worship Jesus in His suffering, a divine and pure suffering, such as the earth has never seen.

Suffering that is fed by fervent, tender love.

Suffering completely free from self.

Suffering of abysmal depths, such as no man has ever endured.

Suffering full of glory, nobler than any suffering of man.

Suffering that Jesus bore in all weakness with such strength, uttering those courageous words, "Thy will be done!"

Suffering that Jesus endured with a truly childlike attitude, entreating the disciples to stand by Him and beseeching the Father, "If it be possible, let this cup pass from me."

Suffering that Jesus underwent with but two words on His lips, "My Father, My Father!"

Suffering that resulted in Satan's downfall, for here was Someone who suffered humbly as a Child of the Father, submitting to the will of God and His blows.

Suffering that dealt the fatal blow to Satan, the rebel who strove to attain greatness and to set up his throne above the heavens.

Let us, therefore, worship Jesus for His suffering in Gethsemane with songs of praise and adoration. Let us worship Him in a spirit of deep shame that in this age of rebellion we so grieve Jesus when as His own we do not bear suffering in childlike trust and say ever anew, "Yes, Father!" Let us worship Jesus as sinners and humble ourselves beneath the blows of God, for we deserve chastening.

Let us worship Jesus and in deep shame confess that we are so quick to cease loving others when they inflict suffering upon us, hurt or disappoint us, whereas Jesus never ceases to love His disciples.

But let us also praise and adore Jesus, firmly believing that through His pure, divine suffering He has redeemed us from our reluctance to bear our cross. Yes, we believe that our Lord Jesus will now ennoble our suffering and help us to bear it in love and humility with a childlike attitude, well-pleasing to the Father, as the fruit of Jesus' suffering in Gethsemane.

all sing

> O Love beyond comparing
> That went through pain and night!
> To win for us salvation,
> Lord, You went forth to die.
> My Jesus, how You suffered
> In deepest agony
> As You with Satan struggled
> There in Gethsemane!

O let us sing Your praises
A thousand, thousandfold.
'Twas we, O Lord, who left You
In misery untold.
In Your distress and anguish
You had to plead alone.
Your prayers to God the Father
Ne' er seemed to reach His throne.

O joy! The foe was vanquished
There in Gethsemane!
The vict'ry was accomplished
Through Your soul's agony,
Which You, Lord, disregarded
In Your great love for men.
You only sought to save us,
To ransom us from sin!

melody WJ 52 or
"The Church's One Foundation"

JESUS' FIRST BATTLE IN GETHSEMANE

We can imagine that Satan, full of scorn, may have shown Jesus here the vastness of the sin He intended to take upon Himself. How dreadful it must have been for Jesus to see the atrocity of all sins, with the burdens and punishments they incur, from the Fall of man to the end of the world — and to taste them that hour!

What revulsion fills us sinful men, especially today in the last times when we hear of all the sins and crimes that cover the earth like the waves of the sea and pervade all the nations like a pestilence! How we shudder when we hear of the inhuman methods used in the murder of millions of unborn children, when we hear of the crimes, acts of violence and gruesome murders committed daily — even by children — when we hear of the filthiest sins of licentiousness and the most repugnant instances of blasphemy! Our hearts almost break when we hear that even children are becoming ill or harmed for life as a result of drug-addiction, alcoholism and licentiousness, and that Satanism is spreading like wildfire across the earth with its outrageous blasphemy. Terrible torture is inflicted upon Christians in prison camps. At all this we can only cry aloud, "O the horrors of sin — sin, which breeds misery, guilt and destruction! How vile and infernal it is!"

Perhaps this gives us a dim impression of that which Jesus must have suffered in Gethsemane. He experienced the horrors of sin not only of one age or one nation in the manifold manifestations of sin and wickedness. No, the vulgarity, malice and perversion of all times in their thousandfold repulsiveness were laid upon Him.

And this He suffered not as a sinner like us but as the Son of God who knew no sin. What abysmal dread must have gripped Him when He saw the vileness of sin!

choir

> A Lamb bears all man's wickedness,
> Which grows despite Christ's graciousness,
> Heaps up as high as mountains.
> God's heart is heavy with distress
> And like a mighty host sins press
> Upon His soul to crush Him.

speaker

> And day by day man's sins increase
> Till almost all the Father sees
> Is wickedness and evil.

23

Mankind bears Satan's image now,
Depraved, corrupt — yet who speaks out?
God's tears alone are flowing.

choir

Your heart is heavy, Lord most dear,
But lo, Your bride comes to You here.
She yearns to suffer with You,
To share the burden, wrestle, pray,
That many will turn home, be saved,
And bring You joy and comfort.

In Gethsemane it was Satan's intention to torment Jesus by showing Him the sins of us men. Jesus may have cried out in His heart when He saw the abysmal horrors of sin. Satan tormented Jesus by even accusing Him of being the cause of sin, as the Pharisees had maintained. Satan reproached Him, saying that He had caused confusion and disorder by breaking up families and taking away their peace. He also claimed that Jesus had brought nothing but contention, since He did not uphold the old customs and this caused such unrest in both the religious and secular life of the people. Satan blamed Jesus for the massacre of the innocent children in Bethlehem and held Him responsible for the suffering of His parents, who were forced to flee to Egypt. And he accused Him of many other things.

If we consider an example from our personal lives, we may have an inkling of Jesus' temptations in Gethsemane. For instance, in response to a call to serve God we may have broken family ties for Jesus' sake. Such a step may have caused much heartache and someone may have even fallen ill as a result. Then we too hear the voice of temptation, "You were to blame! If this leading has caused such distress, how could it possibly be of God? You were supposed to bring love and joy, but instead you have brought misery!"

But far deeper and beyond all comparison must have been the anguish of our Lord Jesus, whose heart was filled with tender love and who did nothing else but bring love to His children in order to make them happy. What pain and distress Jesus must have undergone in that hour when He was accused of causing so much devastation, discord and distress because of His words and claims on us! What torment Jesus must have suffered to be accused of being the cause of so many offences and so much misery!

Jesus wrung His hands and broke out in a cold sweat; He was trembling und shuddering. As He struggled to raise Himself, His knees shook and His legs were scarcely able to hold Him. He was completely disfigured and the colour had left His lips after this first battle had been waged. Though barely able to stand upright, Jesus forced Himself to walk. Swaying, He made His way to the three disciples. And how did He find them? Huddled together, one resting his head on his arm, the other leaning against the chest of the third. Exhausted, deeply troubled, fear-stricken — asleep in temptation. Jesus, though He Himself was in the utmost anguish, now approached the disciples as the Good Shepherd, who tends His flock knowing it to be in danger. But He also came as someone in extreme trepidation, driven by horror to seek His friends.

Let us worship Him in His suffering love and express our gratitude by singing:

all sing

> Love that grieved on Mount of Olives,
> Weeping, sweating blood for me!

25

Ever yearning, ever longing,
Love that loved unceasingly!
Love that bore God's holy anger
With all heart and mind and will!
Love that by its very dying
Stilled the wrath that none could still!

cf. *Altes bayrisches Gesangbuch* 124
can be sung to the melody, "Love
Divine, All Loves Excelling"

Up till that point the disciples had shared in Jesus' power, in His miracles, in His loving care and in His glory — and now they were to take part in His fear and agony. Later they were even to share His sufferings and suffer on His behalf. But Jesus found them sleeping. They were not sharing His grief. Disappointed and full of sorrow over His disciples, Jesus said to Peter, "Simon, are you asleep?" In His abandonment Jesus lamented, "Oh, could you not watch with Me even one hour?"

choir

O Jesus alone
In sorrow and woe!
Alone in temptation's garden
And not a soul heeds Your affliction!

Who stands by Your side
In Your greatest plight? —
Forsaken by God, by Your children!
For sinners God now makes atonement!

Jesus, Lord and King, Creator of heaven and earth, stands before His disciples here — pale, disfigured, trembling, swaying and bathed in perspiration.

Who can fathom such abasement of Jesus, the Lord God, the second Person of the Godhead? Oh, it is scarcely comprehensible! And yet not one of the disciples stood by Jesus in His untold agony. The disciples were only dismayed and distressed to see their strong Master now standing so frail and disfigured before them. Was not Jesus the Lord and Master at whose word even the wind and the waves were stilled? Now they felt forsaken. Perhaps they thought that Jesus had lost His mind.

He had sustained them; He had been their sole support. But now, as the enemy drew close, they felt robbed of all security. Their support was taken from them. Whom could they turn to now? They were paralyzed with grief, distress and despair, because they had not consented to the cross and the path that would lead to suffering, cross-bearing and death. Consequently, they had but one desire — to suppress the reality of their terrible disappointment and suffering. They wished neither to hear nor see any more of this. All they wanted to do was sleep!

Oh, if only they had made their committal beforehand! Then Jesus' words would have been in their hearts, "And on the third day the Son of man will be raised." They would have been consoled, knowing that with Jesus suffering and the cross would not be the final outcome. In the midst of their affliction they would have found the strength to say, "Yes, Father" and this would have immersed their hearts in peace. They would not have lost their trust in God or failed in the hour of temptation. But now they were defeated.

Deeply disappointed, Jesus returned to His cave. In vain had He waited for comfort, sympathy and a loving word. He was unable to share any of His grief and sorrow with His disciples — they were unreceptive.

And how often Jesus suffers the same disappointment in His disciples today! Our NO to suffering has serious consequences — we forsake Jesus in the very situations that call for our loyalty. This is what is happening today when Jesus is so derided and the world is filled with blasphemies.

Today Jesus is waiting for disciples to stand by Him and to stand up for Him, disciples who out of love for Him are willing to share His disgrace and accept suffering with a "Yes, Father".

all pray

> My Jesus, here will I kneel beside You
> At this rock of Your fear and agony.
> Out of love will I stay with You
> When You lead me through the dark valley.
> I will stay by You. I will endure to the end with You,
> Prepared to battle through the darkest night
> Until You lead me home to dwell with You,
> To live in glory and eternal light.

Inscription
in the Gethsemane Grotto, Canaan

JESUS' SECOND BATTLE IN GETHSEMANE

This time Jesus fell down upon His face. Perhaps He was shown to what extent He would have to suffer in atonement for the sins of the world. What untold agony this must have caused Jesus! He saw into the abyss of every sin, recognizing the nature and implication of all sinful desires and the terrible effect they have on the human soul and body.

How dreadful it would be if we had to take a glimpse into the abyss of sin! Then we would see that every sin destroys a particular trait of God's image in our soul, spirit or body and makes us sick and ugly. No words can express the terrible power sin exercises over body, soul and spirit and the devastating effects it has on them.

That hour in Gethsemane Jesus could see the immeasurable heartache caused by sin and the punishment it incurs. Do we ever consider that all wars are born out of the sin of hatred? What grief they bring to thousands and millions when women lose their sons and husbands! Do we also realize that the sin of escapism, of unwillingness to suffer, leads to addictions? Through drugs, for instance, countless numbers of people in the flower of their youth have ruined their lives.

It is impossible to describe the devastating effects that sin has had upon our world, and the chastisement and torment it inflicts upon us even in this life.

*Jesus could also see the instruments of torture used down through the ages since the beginning of the world. He could see the inquisitions, the concentration camps, the torture inflicted upon those persecuted for His sake. He could visualize the different types of cruelty invented by human fury and wickedness for the torture of men. It is the height of sin when men enjoy torturing others. Jesus could see what agony it would cost Him to atone for all of this, and His sweat became like drops of blood.

Satan himself may have staged the next attack by placing the agonizing question in Jesus' heart, "What will be the gain, the fruit of My sacrifice?"

Visions of a terrible future may have oppressed Jesus' heart. In spirit He may have seen the future sufferings of the apostles and the small host of believers of the Early Church. The words, "in vain" must have resounded loudly in His soul.

He saw that many heresies would arise in His Church,

His Body. He saw that in spite of His act of redemption the entire Fall of man would be repeated through the pride, disobedience, vanity, self-righteousness, luke-warmness, wickedness and sinful desires of countless numbers of baptized Christians, who would bear His name on their lips. He may well have seen proud teachers of the Gospel with their manifold lies and deceitful reasoning, and many a sinful life under a pious cloak. Jesus could see the apostasy of His Church, the "abomination of desolation" in the Kingdom of God on earth and the ingratitude of man, whom He was about to ransom with His lifeblood in immeasurable suffering.

Satan presented several frightening pictures to Jesus, showing how he would snatch souls who had been saved by His blood and strangle them before His eyes. Indeed, in this hour Jesus was shown how His bitter death of atonement would be abused.

Then Satan, the Tempter, whispered to Him, "Do you really want to suffer for such ingratitude?" In an agony Jesus wrung His hands — the powers of darkness pressed in upon Him so closely that His sweat fell as drops of blood upon the earth. How He was tormented at the thought of undergoing immeasurable suffering for such an unthankful world!*

choir

> Tormented Your soul
> In darkness untold,
> Completely alone and forsaken,
> Assailed by the fury of Satan!

> "Where will My path lead
> Midst hell's tyranny?",
> Your tormented soul asks in anguish.
> The light seems for ever extinguished!

It is shattering to think that Jesus' sweat fell upon the ground as drops of blood when He thought of us, of all those who would one day believe in Him. What agony it must have meant for Jesus to see our ingratitude and our abuse of His bitter death of atonement, to see that we would not love Him with a pure, devoted and undivided heart! What a grief it must have been for Him in that hour to see that we would time and again offer our hand to Satan, His adversary, since we would not renounce sin wholly, but treat it lightly and play with it!

What a battle it was for His human will to overcome the reluctance to undergo such immeasurable suffering for such unworthy beings!

all pray

Lord Jesus,

Long ago You suffered because of the great ingratitude of Your disciples and today it is the same. Therefore it is our heart's desire, ever anew to demonstrate our gratitude for Your agonizing suffering by our actions.

We believe that You will help us to be a joy for You. Grant us this fervent plea, so that we may not grieve You by our ingratitude.

We pray, Lord Jesus, that Your suffering will not be in vain for us and that heaven and hell will witness in our lives what fruit Your suffering yields. In faith in Your act of redemption and in love and gratitude for Your dreadful battle in Gethsemane we no longer want to tolerate our sin. Instead we want to battle against it, to hate it and break with it. Our whole lives shall be a thank offering — You shall not hear a single word of defiance from us when You lead us along hard paths. Lord Jesus, You shall not be disappointed in us. The Accuser shall not be able to say to You, "Your suffering for them was of no avail!" With all our hearts we pray that Your agony in Gethsemane will truly bear fruit in our lives.

Amen.

*In the throes of this inhuman anguish and filled with revulsion at the thought of the horrors that lay before Him, Jesus cried to the Father, "Father, if this cup cannot pass from Me, may Your will be done." Like a man bowed down beneath a heavy burden and about to collapse at any moment, Jesus came to His disciples for the second time. They were sitting hunched over, their covered heads resting on their knees. Again they had fallen asleep in their distress, fear, inner conflict and weariness. But as Jesus now approached them, trembling all over, they sprang up. In the moonlight they saw His bent figure and His pale, blood-stained face gazing at them. He was indescribably disfigured and at first they did not recognize Him. But then they rushed to His side, took His arms and supported Him like loving friends. Yet in their grief and consternation at His appearance and words they did not know what to say or think.

Jesus wanted to return to His cave, but He was so weak that James and John had to lead Him, the King of all worlds.

The other eight disciples were also dismayed and considerably shaken. They were undergoing severe temptation. As they searched for a hiding place, anxious thoughts harassed them. "What shall we do if He is killed? We have left behind all that was ours, we have given up everything, we are poor, the laughing-stock of the world. We had relied on Him. But how helpless and broken He is now! What comfort can He offer us? Oh, what shall we do?"*

The disciples only thought about themselves; they were not concerned about Jesus in His dreadful agony, for they did not yet love Jesus in truth.

Today when one piece of appalling news supersedes the other, when we hear of new instances of blasphemy, of more Christians falling away and of preliminary measures for future persecution against Christians — whom do we think of first?

O Lord Jesus, hear our prayer:

> Jesus, Lord, to love You only —
> I shall live for this alone,
> To Your sad heart comfort bringing,
> All Your suff'ring making known.
>
> Naught I care now for my troubles,
> Since I've seen Your grief and woe.
> Living only to console You,
> Paths of suff'ring I will go.

see WJ 231

JESUS' THIRD BATTLE IN GETHSEMANE

*After returning to His cave, Jesus said, "My Father, if thou art willing, remove this cup from me; nevertheless not my will, but thine, be done."

In the last stage of His battle in Gethsemane, the deepest anguish for our Lord Jesus may have been that He was shown all of His coming suffering bit by bit, from the kiss of Judas to His last words on the cross. He could see the flight of His disciples, the contempt and ill-treatment before Annas and Caiaphas, Peter's denial, the trial before Pilate, Herod's mockery, the scourging, the crowning with thorns, the pronouncing of the death sentence, the procession along the Via Dolorosa where He bore the burden of the cross, His falling beneath the cross, the executioners' ridicule, the brutal nailing to the cross, the upraising of the cross amid the Pharisees' derision, and the grief of Mary, Mary Magdalene and John. All these scenes were shown to Him in detail, including His shameful nakedness on the cross. And He besought the Father for help.

After all these pictures of His suffering had passed before Him, Jesus fell down upon His face like a dying man. His sweat began to flow rapidly. It was now pitch black in the cave, but the last battle in Gethsemane was over.*

choir

> I thank You, Lord, for suff'ring agony,
> That I one day Your countenance may see.
>
> I thank You, Lord, that in Gethsemane
> You fought and vanquished Satan's hosts for me.
>
> I thank You, Lord. You won the victory
> To set me free from sin eternally.

melody WJ 93

An angel held in his hands a chalice and Jesus drank from it. Perhaps the solace contained in this chalice was that the Father gave Jesus a glimpse into the kingdom of the dead, where so many souls were awaiting His arrival, yearning for Him to redeem them. This must have encouraged His loving heart. Or perhaps an angel showed Him all the hosts of future overcomers, who would be the fruit of His suffering and redemptive death that lay before Him and whose lives and ministries would be crowned with victory. Did He perceive what glory His suffering would yield?

Let us imagine that those who would be redeemed by His blood passed before His eyes — a royal host, shining forth the image of God, mirroring the Son's beauty. A host reflecting the image of Jesus, resplendent and radiant with love. A host clothed in wedding garments, crowned and magnificently adorned — the Bride of the Lamb. What an encouragement and consolation such a sight must have been for Jesus!

But today Jesus grieves to see the countless numbers who call themselves by His name and yet in spite of His death continue to live in envy, discord and irreconciliation and yield to sinful desires, as if they had never been redeemed — a distortion of His image. Therefore, let us ask the Lord:

all pray
Our Lord Jesus,

Imprint Your image upon us, Your image of merciful love, of meekness, humility and purity, so that Your heart, which is so often disappointed by Your own, can rejoice over us when You find Your image in us.

We no longer want to tolerate sin, which clings to us so closely and impedes us. We want to fight against it even to the point of shedding blood, calling upon Your victorious name, so that we shall overcome.

We commit ourselves to You, Lord Jesus. Take our will and all that we have. We give our consent to bear the cross and to endure humiliations and chastenings, that we may be transformed into Your image and bring joy to You by our dedication.

Amen.

* Jesus had freely accepted the cup of suffering and had received strength. Though still sorrowful, He was supernaturally strengthened, so that now He could approach His disciples for the third time — with a firm step and without a trace of fear or agitation. He walked upright and with determination. He had dried His face and smoothed His hair, which hung together in strands, damp with cold sweat.

In the meanwhile Judas was drawing near with a band who would take Jesus captive.*

JESUS' ARREST

choir

A prisoner is Jesus, in chains stands the Lord;
O mourn that we sinners such shame on Him poured!
His chains are more cruel than what thieves had to wear —
Our pure, sinless Lord, whom the saints all revere.

He brought only freedom, release to mankind.
And yet He's held captive in chains — doomed to die!
He brought others freedom, salvation and light,
But where is His pow'r now in this darkest night?

O King stripped of power! In chains is pure Love! —
Deprived of the splendour that You owned above!
O Lord, whom all heaven once served willingly,
You now freely choose but a prisoner to be.

A prisoner! A prisoner! O bitter the cry!
A captive of sinners, condemned now to die,
God's very own Son, who created us all,
Who guides and sustains both the mighty and small.

melody WJ 55

My Saviour goes to suffer,
Belovèd Lamb of God.
O let me stay close by You
And share Your way, dear Lord.
Because of me You suffered
And for my sake You died.
Let me lament my sinning
And stay close by Your side.
O let me now go with You,

My dearest Lord and King;
Filled with contrition join You
In Your night of suffering.

The mob, headed by Judas, the traitor, now drew near.
The hour of darkness had come. Jesus would be betrayed
by one of His twelve disciples and delivered into the
hands of His enemies to be put to death. Day in and
day out, for three years, Judas had shared the life of his
Lord. He had known Him as the omnipotent Son of
God and daily experienced Jesus' overflowing love for
him. What a moment of bitter agony it must have been
for Jesus when the evil face of Judas neared Him and
he placed the treacherous kiss upon His lips! Jesus must
have shuddered, but nevertheless He spoke to him in His
amazing, saving love and in His ineffable majesty, "My
friend, why are you here?" And at that moment the
guards closed in on Jesus.

How did they find Jesus in the Garden of Gethsemane? He was no longer trembling and shaking, no
longer a pitiful sight for man. Only His closest and most
trusted followers were permitted to see Him in such
degradation — the ones who had also witnessed His
transfiguration. In His tender love the Father made
Jesus strong now when He had to appear before His
captors and later before the eyes of many. Here at the
beginning of Jesus' path of sorrows the Father enabled
Him to exert His authority once more and demonstrate
to His persecutors who it was that they had come to
capture. It became evident to all present that Jesus was
submitting to this arrest voluntarily, as He had declared
in the Temple in the hearing of many, "I have power
to lay down my life, and I have power to take it again."
Thus Jesus majestically stepped forth and asked the

guards, "Whom do you seek?" And He uttered those kingly words, "I am he! If you seek me, let these men go." At the power of His words the soldiers sank to the ground, unable to act.

And when Peter cut off Malchus' ear, Jesus healed it as a sign that He is truly Lord and that He alone has might.

But then the incredible occurs. Jesus, the Lord of power and might, surrenders Himself to His persecutors and enemies, and they place Him in chains. A deeply moving sight — in eternal majesty, Jesus stands there with bound hands, His appearance and very nature stamped by the graciousness of love and humility. Divine peace emanates from the Lord of lords, who now stands as a prisoner before His sneering enemies, the Pharisees. In full dedication to suffering and the way of the cross, Jesus submits to the power of His enemies. O let us worship this sacred act of the one true Lord, who permits Himself to be bound, although He alone is independent of all things as the Creator of the universe. Let us worship Him for His love, which constrains Him to take this path. It is love for us that makes Him not regard the suffering of captivity!

O Jesus, Love eternal, who can compare with You?

all sing

> Jesus, in fetters bound,
> Why jostled thus around?
> Man always wants to be free,
> Free e'en to disobey
> Whatever God may say,
> All fett'ring bonds tears away.
>
> Jesus now shows to me,
> Though bound, we can be free;

Christ pioneering the way.
All that His Father willed
Jesus in love fulfilled
To set us free from our chains.

Bound as a lamb He's led,
Crucified in our stead;
Watch how He goes to His death.
Lo, God in fetters see;
He waits for those who'll be
Willing to wear chains like Him.

WJ 57

It is as if Jesus were now standing before us as a prisoner in ineffable majesty and humility and saying to us, "Come, take your place at My side! Let yourselves be bound like Me when you want to rule, to make your own decisions and cling to your right of freedom. Turn your eyes upon Me, the Captive, when you are tempted to revolt against regulations or religious commitments, when you are unwilling to obey and submit to authority, when you want to be independent. Relinquish your claims and desires voluntarily. Follow Me now into captivity by giving up opportunities to exert power, so that you will be prepared to enter real captivity with Me in the coming time of persecution when your persecutors seek to imprison you for My name's sake."

all pray

Help me to behold You as the Lamb bound in chains. Jesus, I ask You to prepare me for the time of persecution. Make me like unto You now, that I may be fully surrendered, letting others rule over me, willing to submit to them and to be subject to those who have power and might over me.

Let me be Your little lamb, silently submitting to the will of God, humbly following You however and wherever You lead me, even if You allow me to be led into prison or deported to a labour camp as Your disciple. I will go with You.

Grant that now in everyday life I may have Your image before me, my Lord and Saviour bound in chains, so that I may be prepared for the hour when I must begin to walk Your path of captivity before the visible and invisible world.

Then by Your grace let me be strong like You and say, "Here I am." Grant that Your humility, love and peace will shine forth from me.

Amen.

The mob that had come to arrest Jesus in Gethsemane consisted of soldiers from the Temple guard and servants of Annas and Caiaphas. They were armed with swords and spears. At a distance followed disreputable executioners and uncouth court servants, carrying ropes and chains, and behind them came several officials. With great barbarity and brutality they bound Jesus' hands while the Pharisees made their insolent and derisive remarks. Gruesome and merciless, they tied the hands of our Lord with new, sharp-cutting ropes. Then a spiked belt of chains was placed round His waist, and round His neck they put a halter, which was studded with spikes and other lacerating material. They fastened four long ropes to the belt, so that they could pull our Lord Jesus backwards and forwards in their malevolence. With that the gruesome procession set out from Gethsemane through the Kidron Valley.

What now occurs is almost beyond human understanding. Our Lord Jesus must make His way alone through the Kidron Valley, the vale of tears, of suffering and torment.

The procession must first have passed by the place where Jesus had warned His disciples on the way to Gethsemane. Scarcely a few hours had elapsed. But now Jesus walked the same way in chains, this time alone, without His disciples. They had fled when the cross loomed before them and Jesus was taken prisoner. Suffering had unmasked them and revealed their true colours — they were prisoners of their ego. This is why they could not take Jesus' part and enter captivity with Him. In their dread of the cross and their egoism they proved to be cowards and weaklings.

To this day the Kidron Valley speaks of the procession it witnessed. There has never been one like it. Maltreated and derided, Jesus was pulled with ropes and driven like a beast to the slaughter. No longer was He surrounded by His disciples as in previous years; only wicked executioners were at His side now. In the distance the disciples wandered about, not knowing what to do. Completely distraught, they wept and lamented, and yet they did not have the courage to enter suffering, to surrender their freedom and lives. They had left their Master and Lord to walk His path of affliction alone.

Thus, abandoned by His own, Jesus had to endure the suffering alone on His way through the Valley of Kidron. A cry of lament seemed to fill the Kidron Valley, "No one — no, not one — wants to go with Him; no one wants to stand by Him in suffering; no one wants to give up his freedom to Jesus." As it was long ago, so it is today.

> He goes alone, for none dares with Him go,
> The angels weep, their Maker's fate to know.

Humbly, submissively, He treads this way,
As though for His own sins our Lord must pay.

choir

Jesus, I would not forsake Thee,
But in suff'ring take Thy part.
Make me one with Thee completely,
Place Thy sorrows in my heart.
Unto death, Lord, I will follow!
May my life's oblation be
To go with Thee, dearest Jesus,
Never more forsaking Thee.

melody WJ 69

*The executioners vented all their malice on Jesus, mainly in their base desire to curry favour with the officials, who were full of rage and spite towards Jesus. Still clutching the ropes that held Jesus, the executioners pushed Him down into the Kidron Brook and taunted Him with swear words, telling Him to drink His fill. Only divine support saved Him from injuring Himself fatally. Jesus fell down and they pulled Him out of the water again and lashed Him with knotted ropes like a butcher driving cattle to slaughter. All this took place amid coarse jesting and mockery.

Next the procession led up the other side of the Kidron Brook to Mount Zion. Since the way was narrow and rugged at this point, Jesus was barbarously driven forward with blows and curses, and made to tread on sharp stones, thorns and thistles. The soldiers had a special staff for tormenting that they used to prod and poke Him. And when His bare feet were torn by the stones, thorns and thistles, His heart was wounded by the sarcasm of the Pharisees, who never left His side. Laughing derisively, they would call out, "His forerunner, John the Baptist, certainly didn't prepare the way very well for him here" and "Malachi's prophecy, 'Behold, I send my messenger to prepare the way before me' is not being fulfilled now."

The procession wound its way uphill, arriving first at the small city district called Ophel, the Mount Zion of King David's day. (The house of Annas and Caiaphas, to which they were leading Jesus, stood on the present Mount Zion.) As they approached Ophel, a new troop of soldiers arrived, and while they were passing through Ophel they were joined by a unit of several hundred men. Judas, the traitor, had warned the chief priests that the residents of Ophel were Jesus' most loyal adherents. Most of them were poor workmen, day-labourers, hewers of wood and drawers of water for the Temple. Here Jesus had taught and healed many of the poor labourers, consoled them and given them alms.

The procession now reached the top of the hill and a heart-breaking cry went up as the people of Ophel, who were devoted to Jesus in their deep gratitude, met the procession. Only with great difficulty did the soldiers manage to hold back the crowds of people that were streaming from all sides. Men and women cried with outstretched hands, "Let this man go! Give Him back to us! Who else can help us? Who else can heal and comfort us? Give Him back to us!" It was a heart-rending sight. Jesus was pale, disfigured and bruised, His hair hanging in strands, His dishevelled garments soaked and mud-stained. He was pulled by ropes and prodded with sticks like some poor, half-dazed beast about to be sacrificed. Insolent executioners and boisterous soldiers dragged Him through the streets of Ophel.

How moving it was to see the gratitude of the lamenting people of Ophel! The hands that He had healed of paralysis were stretched out to Him. The tongues that He had loosed called out after Him. The eyes whose sight He had restored followed Him and wept bitterly.*

The people of Ophel were the only ones who filled the Kidron Valley with their cries of lamentation. They were the only ones, because their grateful hearts could not bear to see Jesus undergo such suffering. Not fearing the soldiers, they forced their way to Jesus. The people of Ophel, who were probably not very religious, had the courage to confess their allegiance to Jesus, a courage inspired by love, which is prepared to suffer for the beloved. In contrast Jesus' disciples, to His great sorrow, were not at His side in the hour of His suffering. They did not accompany Him, nor did they weep with Him. Today Jesus is waiting for disciples, for people who will show Him love and thanksgiving by their willingness to bear ridicule, scorn and blows with Him.

Today a new hour of suffering has dawned for Jesus — His Passion on a world-wide scale. Once again Jesus must undergo the painful experience of being forsaken. Countless numbers are abandoning Him and no longer sharing His path, even those who had been in His service for many years and dedicated their lives to Him. In all parts of the world the great apostasy has begun. Once more Jesus is held prisoner — this time in the webs of human views and thinking. Man declares Him powerless and dead and yet attacks Him with hatred and blasphemy. Thus the time has come for Jesus' disciples too to be persecuted and taken captive as He was. Today His words are becoming true, "They will deliver you up to tribulation, and put you to death; and you will be hated by all nations for my name's sake" (Matthew 24:9). Today Jesus is waiting to see which of His disciples will go into captivity with Him.

Today Jesus is looking at us, His disciples, to see

who is ready to suffer imprisonment because of his loyalty to God's commandments. Today He is looking into our hearts to see whether we continually practise yielding our wills and sacrificing them to God when His will brings us suffering, so that we shall then be able to endure suffering when our persecutors come. He entreats us not to forsake and deny Him when that moment comes. Therefore, He asks us to surrender ourselves and our wills today, accepting suffering whenever we are confronted with hardships, difficult leadings and burdens, so that we shall be strong when we are led into suffering, persecution and imprisonment. Then we shall be able to repeat the words of the Apostle Paul, "I am ready not only to be imprisoned but even to die for the name of the Lord Jesus" (Acts 21:13).

choir

> I bind myself to You, to You alone,
> To Your commandments, to Your way.
> O now Your hand upon me lay.
> I'll follow, follow You,
> You are my great reward.
> I'll follow, follow You,
> My Sov'reign and my Lord.

WJ 58

all pray

Jesus, take my will, take my life. Do with me as You please, whether Your will brings me joy or suffering, life or death. I want to remain united with You by surrendering my will and submitting to those whom You have placed over me in everyday life today.

What You ordain, I will do. Wherever You lead me, I will go, even if it means arrest, imprisonment and suffering. I want to go with You and stand at Your side, never denying or forsaking You.

Help me to practise now by making ever new acts of committal to suffering, so that my will may be wholly surrendered to You and more and more engrafted in You. Bind me tightly to You and Your will, so that in suffering I shall be bound to You and unable to forsake You, remaining faithful to You even unto death.   Amen.

choir

In love surrender your desires and longings;
And loving, bind yourselves to Jesus' heart alone.
Come, join us as we raise our song;
O Love eternal, we praise and adore.
A prisoner — today You still suffer —
To Calvary's tree You are driven.
O Love eternal, praise be to You!
Where else has such love e'er been found?
O Love, we would suffer with You.

JESUS ON TRIAL BEFORE ANNAS
AND CAIAPHAS

all sing

Dearest Lord Jesus, what have You committed
That You should now so cruelly be convicted?
What is the crime? O Lord, what is the misdeed
Of which You're guilty?

We see You scourged now, crowned with thorns
    and slandered.
Your holy countenance is sore disfigured!
Made to drink gall and nailed upon the hard cross,
You suffer for us!

What could have caused such agony and suff'ring?
O Lord, 'twas I — my sins and evil-doing.
I am the guilty one who made You suffer,
Jesus, dear Saviour!

Strange and astonishing is this chastisement!
The Shepherd for the sheep endures such torment!
The righteous Lord and Master is atoning
The servants' sinning.

cf. EKG 60

Jesus, driven to the judges
To be tried by mortal men!
Mockingly they dare to sentence
God's own pure and sinless Son!

Dearest Lord, O Man of Sorrows,
I would ever go with Thee.
'Twas I, through my criticizing,
That caused Thee such agony.

That which the Gospels express in brief words about the suffering endured by our Lord Jesus on trial may have taken place the way it was once described:

*It must have been after midnight when Jesus was brought into the palace of Annas and Caiaphas to be tried and judged — the Son of God placed on trial before man, whom He had created! He was led through a well-lit courtyard into a hall. On a raised platform opposite the entrance sat Annas, surrounded by his advisers. Tugging at the ropes, the guards dragged Jesus up and down several steps as they brought Him to Annas, who could scarcely contain his impatience to see Jesus. He was seething with malicious pleasure, scorn and guile.

And now Jesus, pale and harassed, His head bowed and His hands tied, stood in silence before Annas. A smile played on the lips of this lean old man with a thin beard as though he were entirely ignorant of the proceedings and most astonished to see that Jesus was the announced prisoner. He addressed Him in a sarcastic tone of voice, "So you wish to introduce a new teaching? Who gave you the right to teach? Where did you study? Speak. What is this teaching of yours, which is stirring up everyone?"

Jesus raised His weary head and looking at Annas, He said, "I have spoken openly to the world; I have taught where all the Jews assemble. I have said nothing secretly. Why do you ask Me? Ask those who have heard Me what I said to them. Behold, they know what I said."

At these words of Jesus, Annas' face betrayed his anger and rage, and a scoundrel seeking Annas' favour slapped Jesus loudly on the mouth and cheeks, and said, "Is that how you answer the High Priest?"

Jesus, half-stunned by the force of the blow and pulled back and forth by the court servants, was unable to maintain His balance and fell sideways on to the stairs. At this, derisive hoots, peals of laughter, indignant cries, and swearing broke out in the hall. Mistreating Jesus, the servants hauled Him to His feet. But in a calm voice Jesus said, "If I have spoken wrongly, bear witness to the wrong; but if I have spoken rightly, why do you strike Me?"

Annas now summoned those present to report what they had heard Jesus say. A confused babble of slanderous statements and shouts from the mob ensued, one contradicting the other. Every time the authorities made a comment to the accusations brought forth, the court servants and others who stood nearby jostled, poked and ridiculed Jesus. They all wished to imitate the impudent scoundrel who had slapped Jesus in the face. Jesus swayed to and fro. In the end Annas took a piece of parchment containing accusations against the Lord, rolled it up, put it in a hollow gourd, tied it to a reed, and handed it to Jesus as a mock sceptre.*

O lament, ye heavenly hosts! Lament such human madness! In diabolical arrogance man attacks God Himself. The sinner, who deserves death, heaps his sins upon his Lord and God.

choir

> The One who made and holdeth the world in His
> hand,
> The holy Son of God, is blasphemed throughout
> the land.
> O mourn that man should dare to attack his Lord
> and King,
> To wound his Judge and Maker with scorn and
> mockery.
> O mourn that man should dare slander his
> sov'reign Lord and King!

We humble ourselves before You, O Lord and God, whom we sinful men have accused and condemned, and we thank You for undergoing such treatment for the sake of our sins, so that we may be delivered from our spirit of criticism.

We worship You for exposing Your meek and humble heart to the judges' harsh words of injustice, wickedness and contempt.

Praise be to such love! In silence You stood the trial like a lamb, so that our hearts and minds would be set free from our continual faultfinding, and our lips would learn to utter humble words of merciful love.

Today You stand before us, Lord Jesus, pierced by many arrows of accusations and weighed down with grief as You implore us, "Stop finding fault with others, stop accusing others and heaping reproaches upon them, for you are just as guilty and it is presumptuousness to consider yourselves above others, to be indignant at what they do and to condemn them."

all pray

Our Lord Jesus,

We pray that the immeasurable pain and blasphemy You suffered from the accusations and criticism of the religious people of Your day will convict us when we criticize others, for faultfinding is a diabolical practice, characteristic of Satan, the accuser.

We humble ourselves before You in shame for every time we have censured a brother or sister. You are present in each one of them, and thus we have ultimately passed judgment on You as Annas and Caiaphas did. We have pierced Your heart, for You submitted to judgment and death upon the cross, so that we might be set free from our spirit of criticism, which causes untold damage. We pray, grant us heartfelt contrition over this diabolical sin of faultfinding, so that we may experience redemption, for which You paid such a dear price.

As for ourselves, we pray that You would judge us to the core, Lord Jesus Christ, so that, convicted of our own sins, we shall no longer be able to condemn others as we did before; and when duty calls us to speak, let us do so in a humble, loving spirit.

> O dearest Lord, may I behold You
> As the Lamb who silently
> Stood on trial before the judges.
> I renounce my criticizing,
> Which caused You such grief and torment.
> Now I want to be the one accused.
> > Amen.

*When Annas gave Jesus the hollow gourd containing all the charges as a mock sceptre, he said, "Here is the sceptre of your kingdom. All your titles, honours and rights are contained in it. Take it to the High Priest, so that he can see what your commission and kingdom are and give you the appropriate honours. Bind his hands and conduct this king to the High Priest."

They now bound Jesus' hands across His chest, after securing the mock sceptre firmly in His hands. Laughing, shouting in derision and mistreating our Lord, they led Him out of the hall to take Him to Caiaphas.*

In the midst of such deep disgrace and humiliation Jesus heard only mocking voices. And likewise today He is wounded and ridiculed by millions of voices. Oh that He may receive honour and glory from us who belong to Him! Let us worship Jesus in His true nature and being; let us worship Him as the supreme Majesty, full of glory and divine graciousness, the King of kings.

> Jesus, Lord and mighty King beyond comparing,
> All disgrace that Thou art bearing
> Fades as we now honour Thee.
> Crowned with many crowns of glory,
> Sov'reign Lord o'er countless thrones!
> We worship Thy great majesty.
> All of heav'n the song of glory raises,
> Endlessly retells Thy praises.
> We worship Thee, the Lamb,
> Glory and honour to Thee, the Lamb!

But it was still the hour of Jesus' Passion.

As Jesus was being led to Caiaphas, the swearing and mistreatment continued. Those accompanying Him repeated the contemptuous speeches of Annas in their own manner before the people. All the way Jesus was insulted and maltreated, completely at the mercy of human wickedness, and not one of the many to whom He had shown goodness took His part.

While everyone was blaspheming Him, Jesus looked in vain for His disciples. Their absence deeply wounded His heart. Once again today a time of deep shame has come for Jesus, and His grief is as great as His disgrace, which is universal. Above all, He laments that again so few of His followers suffer with Him and speak out for Him, willing to come under disgrace too.

Today as long ago He must be sighing and lamenting as He asks, "Where are My disciples, who are suffering with Me, who are honouring Me in the sight of everyone in recompense for all My disgrace?"

Let us give Him the response of love.

all sing

Lord, we long to suffer with You
When You are so mocked today;
Love and comfort we would bring You,
Dearest Jesus, in this way.
Lord, we yearn to sing Your praises,
Lauding You, O Son of God,
Holy, pure and fairest Jesus,
Throned above as King and Lord!

Lord, when You are so dishonoured,
We would bear with You the shame,
Not lose heart, for it's an honour
To be humbled for Your name.
We would give ourselves to suff'ring,
By Your side in love to stay,
That our lives may bring You comfort,
Dearest Lord, so mocked today!

can be sung to the melody, "Love Divine, All Loves Excelling"

They now arrived with Jesus at the courthouse of Caiaphas, where the Sanhedrin, the council of the Jews, was assembled. Amid furious, derisive shouts, pushes and jerks, Jesus, whose garment was spattered with filth, was led into the atrium, where a muffled murmuring and muttering of repressed anger replaced the unbridled rage of the rabble. Caiaphas, a thickset man, was flushed with rage as he shouted at Jesus, "Is that you, you blasphemer, disturbing this holy night for us?" The mock sceptre was then taken out of Jesus' hands. Caiaphas read the charges and burst into a tirade of insults and accusations against Jesus, while the court servants and the soldiers standing nearby jostled and pushed our Lord. A number of stormy questions were now hurled at Jesus, who in patient suffering looked straight ahead in silence, without glancing at Caiaphas. The executioners, in their attempt to force Jesus to speak, struck His neck and side, hit His hands and poked Him with sharp instruments.

O Jesus, this is how we treat You today too, for that which we have done to the least of men, including children, we have done to You. We humble ourselves, because we have often misused our authority, lashing out in words and gestures, when we tried to force our will upon those who were reluctant to obey us.

all sing

> My sins, O dearest Saviour,
> Are countless in their number
> Like sands upon the shore.
> 'Twas I and my transgression
> That caused Your sore affliction
> And all the agony You bore.

cf. EKG 64

Once again they presented all the accusations that Jesus had answered a hundred times before: He healed the sick and cast out demons through the devil. He desecrated the Sabbath. He broke the fasts. He stirred up the people. He called the Pharisees a "brood of vipers". He kept company with Gentiles, publicans, sinners and women of ill-repute. He permitted himself to be called a king, a prophet — yes, even the Son of God. He continually spoke of his kingdom. He disputed the legality of divorce. He prophesied the downfall of Jerusalem and pronounced "woes" upon the city. These and many other charges they brought against Jesus.

Perhaps we too have often been unwilling to hear and accept the truth from the mouth of God. Have we closed our hearts as soon as judgment was pronounced over us or our world?

Have we too as "religious people" rebelled against Jesus when we were shown our sins and acted as though nothing were amiss in our lives? Have we too sat in judgment upon our Lord when He did not help us or others the way we thought He should, or when He chastened us or others?

(pause for silent prayer)

all pray

Dear Lord Jesus,

Like the people of long ago, we too rebel against You, Love eternal, and criticize You for Your actions. So often it is we — yes, we who consider ourselves to be devout — who are guilty in this respect. This is Your grief today as long ago.

Forgive us, Lord Jesus, for although You are the essence of eternal love and divine compassion, we so often accuse You of being unmerciful and unconcerned about our personal troubles or the social needs and other problems of mankind.

Forgive us for accusing You when Your leadings seem difficult and incomprehensible to us, and when You give us burdens and crosses to bear. We are truly sorry, for with our complaining we have grieved Your heart. Forgive us that we do not want to accept the truth that we are sinners and need to be chastened for our good.

O Lord, You suffered so much criticism and slander from the religious people long ago. Forgive us for causing You such pain again with our faultfinding and rebelliousness. Above all, forgive us for causing You extreme anguish by unfairly condemning other believers and Christian fellowships in our spirit of criticism. We humble ourselves, for in condemning our brothers and sisters we actually condemn You.

Forgive us for whenever we have not borne unjust reproaches, accusations and slander — especially when they came from other Christians — in silence and patience as You did. As we think of Your great suffering, O Lamb of God, unjustly condemned, we do not want to revile when we are reviled, but rather bear injustice lovingly and silently like a lamb out of love for You and in this way prove ourselves as Your ʳrue followers.

> Dearest Lord, in utter silence
> You endure such blasphemy.
> Though You are the Son of God,
> You bear scorn and mockery.
> Oh, forgive my sins against You,
> Dearest Lord, so sinless, pure.
> Now I yearn to bring You honour;
> Wrongs, reproaches I'll endure.
>
> Amen.

*During the trial before Caiaphas all of Jesus' words and teachings were twisted and put forth as accusations against Him. Time and again the proceedings were interrupted by abusive shouts and mistreatment. With pushes and blows they tried to force a reply from His lips. Only by divine assistance could Jesus survive such torment in order to complete the act of atonement for the sins of the world.

The rage of Caiaphas and the whole council grew, since the testimonies were so confusing and contradictory.

And the amazing patience and silence of the Accused incensed them even more. Others, in contrast, became frightened and conscience-stricken at Jesus' silence.

Caiaphas then stood up, walked down a few steps to Jesus and said, "Have you no answer to make to these charges?" He was annoyed that Jesus did not look at him. Throwing up his hands in a rage, Caiaphas addressed Him in a furious tone of voice, "By the living God I adjure you to tell us whether you are the Christ, the Messiah, the Son of God the Most High."

The tumult was broken by a great silence. And strengthened by God, Jesus said in an awe-inspiring voice, a voice of ineffable majesty, the voice of the eternal Word, "I am. You have said so. And I tell you, soon you will see the Son of man sitting at the right hand of majesty and coming on the clouds of heaven." As Jesus uttered these words, a radiance shone about Him, and the heavens were opened above Him.*

choir

> Come, O come in hosts unnumbered,
> Men, and angels round the throne.
> Come, surround Him, so derided —
> He, the pure and holy Son!
> Soon He will return in glory;
> How His own will praise Him then,
> With great love rejoicing round Him,
> Paying homage without end!

*Caiaphas, however, as though incited by hell, seized the hem of his ceremonial robe, slashed it with a knife, rent the garment with a hissing sound and cried aloud, "He has blasphemed against God! What further testimony do we need? You have heard the blasphemy from his own lips. What do you say?" All the members of the

Sanhedrin that were present rose as one body and cried with a frightening voice, "He deserves death!" And while the shouting was going on, the terrible raging of the powers of hell in the house was at its peak. The enemies of Jesus seemed to be possessed by Satan. Those present who still had some good in their souls were overcome with such horror that many drew their cloaks round them and crept away.

The High Priest then said to Jesus' torturers, "I shall deliver this king into your hands. Give this blasphemer the honour he deserves!" And like a pack of wolves the rabble fell upon our Lord, who until then had been tightly held with ropes by two executioners. With clenched fists the mob rained blows upon Him. They prodded Him with spiked clubs and jabbed Him with needles. In the most shameful fashion they poured out their vulgarity upon our tormented Lord. They took turns putting several different types of mock crowns made of straw upon His head. And then they knocked them off again with spiteful and sarcastic remarks. They cried, "Behold, the son of David with his father's crown!" Or, "Behold, he is greater than Solomon!"

In this way they derided all the eternal truths that Jesus had proclaimed plainly or in parables for the salvation of mankind. They pushed Him from side to side and spat at Him in the most disgusting manner. After they had taken off His handwoven garment, they placed a fool's cap on His head and on top of it a straw wreath.

Jesus now stood there with nothing on but a loincloth and a wrap to cover His neck and chest. But this latter garment they also tore off Him and it was never returned to Him. They dressed Him in an old, tattered cloak, the front of which did not even reach His knees. Round His neck they hung a long iron chain, which reached down from His shoulders, over His chest to His knees. This chain ended in heavy spiked rings, which painfully wounded His knees every time He walked or stumbled. Once again they bound His hands across His chest and shoved a sceptre into His hands. They covered His bruised face with their loathsome spit. His tangled hair and beard, His chest, the whole upper part of His cloak, were caked with all manner of filth. They blindfolded Jesus with a dirty rag, struck Him with their fists and beat Him with sticks, crying out, "Great prophet, prophesy and tell us who hit you!" But Jesus did not utter a word. Instead He prayed silently for His tormentors.

With pushes and blows they dragged Jesus round in a circle before the council, which mocked and insulted Him. It was like a wild, sinister, horrifying scene enacted by envenomed, demon-like characters. Only round the maltreated Lord Jesus could a wonderful radiance often be seen — ever since He had declared that He was the Son of God. The contempt of man could not rob Him of His ineffable majesty.*

all sing

> Who caused You such affliction,
> O Jesus, my Salvation?
> Who wrought such misery?
> O Lord, we and our offspring
> Have sinned from the beginning.
> Yet You have never sinned at all!
>
> 'Twas I, my dearest Saviour.
> I should be made to suffer,
> Bound hand and foot in hell.
> The fetters and the scourging

And all Your bitter suff'ring
My soul, O Lord, deserves to bear.

cf. EKG 64

O Jesus, eternal Son of God, endowed with dignity and majesty, we cannot comprehend it. We can only humble ourselves in the dust before You that not only were You subjected to such humiliation, mistreatment and blasphemy long ago by Your chosen people, but that You are so cruelly derided today in all Christian nations, although they know of Your suffering and Your death upon the cross.

Today You are once again blasphemed most despicably — blasphemed and degraded in innumerable publications, stage and film productions. Our hearts are filled with lamentation over this abysmal sin.

And it is we, the believers, who are usually guilty, for how many Christians attend these blasphemous productions, applaud them and recommend them to others!

Father, forgive us this blasphemy, which is the most serious sin of all. Grant that we may weep in contrition over our coldheartedness and indifference towards You. Forgive us that we can stand by and watch all this happening without longing fervently to show You all the more love and honour, to seize every opportunity to speak out and to do something on Your behalf.

choir

> Jesus, dearest Lord, I pray
> Let me stay with You today,
> Not forsaking You,
> O majestic Lord and King,
> So degraded and blasphemed
> Before all the world.

Long ago, Lord, You were scorned,
Cruelly blasphemed, crowned with thorns
In one land alone.
Now the whole world hates Your name,
Treats You with contempt and shame,
Tormenting Your soul.

choir

At Your side I yearn to stay,
Going with You on Your way,
Though the path be hard.
I will bear with You Your pain,
Persecution, hatred, shame,
O Jesus, my Lord.

all speak

I will take my stand for You
When Your heart is pierced anew
By the darts that fly.
I will testify to You —
God and King to whom is due
All honour and praise!

PETER'S DENIAL

Annas and Caiaphas, Jesus' enemies, had derided Him and tormented Him to the limits of endurance. They claimed that He had a devil and condemned Him for saying that He was the Son of God. In spite of all His grief at such wickedness, these accusations did not surprise Jesus. He knew the Pharisees; they had always been His foes.

But now someone who was closely knit to Jesus in a warm relationship of love, one of His favourite disciples, joined their ranks and declared, "I do not know the man you're talking about." Indeed, cursing himself and swearing, he expressed it even more strongly — and at that Jesus' heart must have almost broken with grief — "I tell you, I don't know the man at all!" In Biblical times this meant, "I renounce this man. I will have nothing to do with him!" And for three years he had been with Jesus day in and day out. Peter said this at a moment when his beloved Lord was in special need of His disciples' love and faithfulness, at a moment when He was so cruelly humiliated, maltreated and derided, forsaken and left at the mercy of evil.

What grief Peter inflicted upon his Lord Jesus with his words! Yet did he not love his Master? Had he not entered the courtyard to be close to Him? He suffered agonies at the way Jesus was being treated. But his love was not pure like that of his Master, who could say, "Yes, Father" in all humility and sincerity. Peter's love was egoistic and filled with self-pity. He lashed out and became a rebel when suffering struck him. This accounts for his remonstration to Jesus but a short while before that, "Heaven forbid, Lord! This shall never happen to You." Now in the hour of testing he had to pay for his lack of dedication to the cross and suffering. Now his dread of suffering was greater than his love. Consequently, he was not prepared to suffer with his Lord, to enter imprisonment and death with Him. Thus he uttered those terrible words of denial, "I do not know the man!"

Peter did not *want* to know Jesus, because Jesus no longer stood before him as the divine, omnipotent Lord that he had known for three years, the Lord who performed signs and wonders and at whose word the dead were raised.

Now Jesus was humiliated, laden with disgrace, wretched and robbed of His dignity. Peter did not want to know a Lord who was under the shadow of the cross, because Jesus' disgrace signified that the cross and suffering also loomed before him. With his denial he pierced the heart of his Lord, which was already heavy-laden with torment, scorn and accusations, for no one can wound us more than someone we love.

O that our Lord Jesus, who was already in extreme anguish, had to suffer such deep wounds inflicted by those who were very close to Him! Long ago it was His disciple Peter; now it is we, His disciples of today. We too do not want to know Him or have anything more to do with Him when He comes to us as the Lord of the cross, the Man of Sorrows, and takes us as His disciples with Him along the path of the cross — yes, into disgrace and even persecution.

How despised our Lord Jesus is! We count Him as nothing. He is worth so little to us that we reject His cross. We turn Him away when He brings the cross into our lives. Yes, we then renounce our discipleship, saying, "I do not know You. I do not know You as the Lord of the cross, nor do I want to know You as such."

Never would Peter forget that inexpressibly sad look that Jesus gave him when He turned His bruised face towards him.

And today when Jesus once more is subjected to the most terrible derision, degradation, scorn and blasphemy even in His Church, how we grieve Him when we do not want to stand at His side when this earns us contempt now and will bring us more and more persecution. How much suffering we inflict upon Jesus when we do not want to accept Him now as He is, the Lord of the cross, and — like Peter long ago — refuse to accept the cross from His hands! Then in the hour when we are called to bear witness to Jesus at the risk of being put on trial and imprisoned, we shall deny Him as Peter did.

In this night of the Passion, when Jesus is in our midst, He is looking at each one of us and asking, "How much am I worth to you? Is your love for Me sincere? That is, are you prepared to suffer for Me?" O that His sad gaze may fall upon us too when suffering strikes us or threatens to come into our lives, so that we shall not say, "May this never happen to me."

Peter wept bitter tears of repentance in response to Jesus' sorrowful gaze. Will Jesus find us shedding such tears about the times we have inwardly rebelled against suffering? If so, we shall be prepared for the time of persecution and able to remain faithful to Him.

Let us remember the times when, as His disciples, we have grieved and bitterly disappointed Jesus by rebelling against our cross. For in our rebellion we did not open our hearts to Jesus in His sufferings, nor wish to stand at His side and carry our cross after Him. In deep contrition let us say:

Jesus, my dearest Lord,
Look now on me,
That I may understand
What I have done to You.
Lord, look on me, as once You did on Peter gaze.
Lord, look on me.

Jesus, my dearest Lord,
Look now on me.
Lord, Your sad look has power,
Can penitence impart,
Preparing me to suffer out of love for You.
Lord, look on me.

Jesus, my dearest Lord,
Look now on me,
That I, like Peter, too
May weep so bitterly,
Love You and not grieve You
   when persecution comes.
Lord, look on me.

JESUS' PATH OF DISGRACE THROUGH JERUSALEM TO PILATE

all sing

> Lord Jesus, may Your fear and pain,
> Your suffering so dreadful
> Ever before my eyes remain,
> That I may shun all evil.
> As long as I have life and breath,
> O Jesus, may Your bitter death
> Be in my contemplation.

> O Lord, You left Your throne on high,
> Came to a place so foreign,
> Were nailed upon a cross to die
> Midst blows and cruel derision,
> So that despite our wickedness
> You might obtain God's grace for us,
> That we might be forgiven.

cf. EKG 69

*Very early the next morning, at the break of day, the chief priests ordered Jesus to be brought out of the dungeon, where He had spent the few remaining hours of the night. They confirmed the verdict they had decided upon in the night — to expel Him from the people of God and thus to have Him put to death by the Gentiles. Accordingly, they brought Him to Pilate in order to obtain the legal death sentence. But even now as they led Jesus to Pilate, they treated Him like a prisoner condemned to death, placing the chain round His neck.

The chief priests and some of the council members led the way. Then came our Lord between the executioners and guards, with the rabble following. The procession descended Mount Zion, entered the lower city, and passed on to Pilate's palace. With ropes cruelly binding Him, our Lord was conducted through the most populated section of the city, which was now teeming with foreigners as well as visitors from all parts of the country who had come to celebrate the Passover.

Jesus was only clad in His undergarment, which was covered with spittle and filth. The long, dangling, large-linked chain hung down from His neck to His knees, striking them painfully as He walked. As on the previous night His hands were tied, and once again the guards led Him by ropes fastened to His belt.*

Wherever Jesus was led, whether it was from Annas to Caiaphas, whether it was through the streets of Jerusalem to Pilate or to Herod, His hands were always bound. In all Jerusalem He was displayed as a criminal who had to be kept in chains.

O let us worship our Saviour in fetters, the King deprived of all power, Love bound in chains. O eternal Majesty of heaven, Ruler of all lands, how weak and powerless You were, bound like a lamb that is led to the slaughter! Yes, Jesus was bound with ropes, because He was to be portrayed as the Lamb. Had not John the Baptist said, "Behold the Lamb of God"? This was the image that thousands of eyes were to see. Thus Jesus was driven like a beast to the slaughter through the many streets of Jerusalem. There all men walked about freely with untied hands; yet He, the one Lord, our Maker, voluntarily submitted to the chains and let Himself be publicly displayed as a prisoner!

Jesus, Jesus, dearest Lamb,
Thou, the Maker of the world,
Bound so cruelly in fetters and chains!
Here I see my sins reflected.
How can I such suff'ring fathom?
Such love I'll ne'er understand!

Jesus, Jesus, dearest Lamb,
Hear my plea, accept my love
In response to Thy suff'ring for us.
I would love Thee, share Thy pathway,
Yield my will to Thee completely,
Who didst bear such bitter pain.

So often during His Passion Jesus portrayed the image of a prisoner, as if He wished to impress this upon our consciences as a perpetual warning for every time we rebel against the will of God when His will runs counter to ours or when it brings us suffering. Indeed, this image of Jesus as He was led through the streets of Jerusalem bound in chains is a powerful challenge and an unmistakable warning. In infinite love He seeks to turn us from all defiance and rebellion against God in this age of revolutions and persecutions; He seeks to draw a "Yes, Father" from our lips, and to move us to surrender our wills in every situation and to dedicate ourselves to suffering, especially to suffering for His name's sake.

Henceforth let us be wholly surrendered to the will of God; let us also submit to it when people are His instruments, for instance, our tormentors in the time of persecution. Out of love for Jesus, the Lamb that was tormented, let us be completely dedicated to the will of God. In this way we shall be a comfort and a joy for

Him. And let us be loyal and follow this pathway of Jesus in the sight of others, even if we incur contempt, ridicule, disgrace, ostracism and persecution. Indeed, let us consider it a privilege to suffer with Him today. Out of love for us Jesus had the courage to endure the jeers and derisive shouts of many. He had the courage to let the people spit at Him, pelt Him with mud and treat Him like the most unworthy, base and despicable man and criminal. And all for love of us.

Along these paths of humiliation Jesus redeemed us from our cowardly nature, which continually seeks the favour of men at the expense of Jesus, whom we often deny in the process, and at the expense of His commandments, which we then often abandon. Now Jesus is waiting for us to follow Him step by step even when it entails entering suffering for His sake. He is waiting for us to be willing to be humiliated, despised and insulted by men for seeking only God's favour and pleasure. If we try to please men, we are no longer servants of Christ, for He walked the path of disgrace; moreover, we shall not have the strength to stand by Jesus when testifying to Him will cost us our freedom or even our lives.

Jesus was disfigured beyond recognition from the terrible mistreatment He received during the night and during this walk through the streets. Amid fresh taunts and cruel blows He was driven on. The riffraff of the crowd was egged on to make a mockery of His royal entry into Jerusalem on Palm Sunday. They jeered at Him, shouting all sorts of royal titles. They threw stones, pieces of wood and dirty rags before His feet and sang derisive songs to Him in mockery of His festive entry into Jerusalem.

How hard it is for us to bear it when people see us humiliated in a weak moment or when some sickness or deformity makes us look ugly! Our Lord Jesus submitted wholeheartedly to such humiliations, so that we might be able to follow His example, especially in times of persecution.

all pray

We humble ourselves before You, Lord Jesus, in shame that we find it so hard to bear humiliation and scorn in our lives, whereas in Your Passion You suffered so much derision and blasphemy and were degraded in the sight of thousands. And yet the disciple should not be above his master!

We now want to stand at Your side and commit ourselves to bear insults and disgrace for Your sake. We want to practise now, so that when the time soon comes for us to meet disgrace, ridicule, scorn and persecution, we shall be able to bear it in Your spirit. Lord Jesus, we pray that You will help us, in the midst of pain to give thanks that we may — in a small way — partake of the untold sufferings and humiliations You underwent as the Lord Most High. No one could be so deeply humiliated, for no one had been so highly exalted.

Forgive us that in our pride we find it so hard to accept disgrace, although as sinners we have deserved it. Forgive us that we are only concerned about ourselves and our reputation when we encounter the smallest insult or humiliation. Forgive us that we cannot bear the slightest scorn or disgrace, that we cannot overcome in such situations, because we are so little moved by the disgrace and blasphemy You had to endure long ago and must suffer once again today.

Amen.

(Let us pause for silent prayer to make an act of dedication and to renounce our dependency upon the praise and opinions of others, our false emotional attachments and our desire for prestige.)

O Lamb, beyond expression
Is Thy humility,
Thy love that ransomed sinners
From all iniquity.
Thy life to us Thou gavest
In death upon the cross,
That we might gain salvation,
Be freed from grief and loss.

O Lamb of God most holy,
I praise and worship Thee!
My life, O Man of Sorrows,
Be Thine entirely.
Henceforth with Thee I'll follow
Thy path of grief and shame,
Standing in love beside Thee
And sharing all Thy pain.

melody WJ 62 or
"The Church's One Foundation"

After Jesus' walk of humiliation through His city, surely God must be waiting for these same streets to resound with the cries of hosanna to His Son? There where Jesus was disgraced He should now be proclaimed before all as the true Lord of the world, the King of kings! In the measure that we love Him will His shame burn in our hearts, so that we have no peace until He is honoured also in Jerusalem, His city. When the praises of Mohammed ring out across the roofs and streets of this city several times a day, should not the praises of Jesus resound even more from His own, from hearts filled with love and thanksgiving? As Christians we have special reason to do so, since we have amends to make.

After Jesus was led in disgrace through Jerusalem, this city witnessed another procession — the entry of the Crusaders, who as Christians brought new disgrace and scorn upon the name of Jesus by causing a terrible blood-bath here.

Today we Christians travel to so many different countries for our own enjoyment, but is it not sad that often we do not have the desire to travel to the place where Jesus suffered? There in Jerusalem at the sites of Jesus' sufferings, should He not be honoured by thousands and comforted by our love in response to all His disgrace?[1]

In the city of Jerusalem, where Jesus was crucified, should He not be honoured throughout the year — not only on Palm Sunday? What a testimony it would be if a group of Christians whose hearts are aflame to pay homage to their King descend the Mount of Olives every Sunday singing songs of adoration on the way to the city!

Indeed, may our hearts be gripped by a fervent desire to bring our Lord Jesus Christ more adoration as a foreshadowing of the true royal procession that will take place one day. And if we do not have the opportunity of doing so in Jerusalem itself, let us use every opportunity elsewhere to glorify Him, sing of Him and bear testimony to Him, painting a picture of Him to others who do not know Him, so that they too may come to believe in Him and give Him glory.

---

[1] Information about pilgrimages to the Holy Land with the Evangelical Sisterhood of Mary is available upon request.

O honour, yes, honour the Lamb now be given,
As great as the shame that He once received.
His own now surround Him with honour
    and crown Him,
Adoring the Godhead for evermore!

melody WJ 245

Glory to the Lamb, glory to the Lamb,
Glory to the Lamb 'throned on high!
Glory to the Lamb, glory to the Lamb,
Glory to the Lamb 'throned on high!
Hallelujah! Hallelujah!
Glory to the Lamb 'throned on high!

Glory, glory, Lord, we offer
Such as we would give no other.
Glory, comfort, love be Yours.

melody WJ 56

JESUS IS TRIED BY PILATE FOR THE FIRST TIME AND MOCKED AT HEROD'S PALACE

all sing

Jesus, Jesus, my Belovèd,
Lamb of God, now glorified,
Once You chose the cross of suff'ring,
Willingly for us You died.
Let me, Lord, with love now follow
On Your path of pain and death;
Let me feel the grief and anguish,
Which You felt at ev'ry step.

Jesus, Jesus, my Belovèd,
How I worship and adore
Such great love, such bitter suff'ring
That You in Your Passion bore!
Let me trace Your holy footsteps
Where You wept in agony.
Let me now my whole life offer,
For You bore such pain for me.

> can be sung to the melody, "Love Divine, All Loves Excelling"

*Jesus was now brought to Pilate, whose palace lay to the northwest of the Temple in a magnificent complex of buildings that included the praetorium, the courthouse and a number of other courtyards and houses.

Jesus was dragged up the long flight of marble steps at the entrance to the palace by the court servants. Pilate, who had heard many a rumour about Jesus, now saw Him standing there so terribly ill-treated and disfigured and yet still giving an impression of immortal dignity.

At this Pilate's contempt for the chief priests and the elders grew, who had informed him that they would deliver Jesus of Nazareth to him to be sentenced, saying that He was guilty of death.

Pilate made it clear to them that he was not inclined to condemn Jesus without proof of His guilt. In an imperious and sarcastic tone of voice, he addressed the chief priests, saying, "What charge do you have to make against this man?" Full of indignation, they retorted, "If we didn't know he was a criminal, we wouldn't have brought him to you." "Take him then," said Pilate, "and judge him according to your law." They replied, "You know that we do not have absolute authority to execute the death sentence."

The Roman governor now demanded that they produce their charges and they brought forward three principal charges against Jesus, each time with a number of witnesses stepping forward to give evidence. They presented their case in such a way as to make Jesus appear guilty of committing a crime against Caesar, so that He would have to be condemned by Pilate; for in matters pertaining only to their religious laws and the Temple, they would have had to pronounce the sentence themselves.

They claimed that Jesus had been subverting the people and that He said they should eat His flesh and drink His blood. Pilate was annoyed at the passionate fury with which they made the accusations. They also accused Jesus of inciting the people and telling them not to pay taxes to Caesar.

As their third main charge they declared that He was a man of lowly and dubious birth, that He had won many adherents and loudly pronounced "woes" over Jerusalem. They said that at one point the people had wanted to make Him King, but He had hidden Himself, since He felt that the time was not yet ripe. But then a few days ago He had held a noisy procession into Jerusalem, permitting the people to pay homage to Him and hail Him with the words, "Hosanna to the Son of David! Praise be to Him who has come to establish the kingdom of our father David!"*

all pray

Lord Jesus,

Because of us and our sins You had to suffer such false accusations. You know if and when we have accused others unjustly or passed on unfavourable and harmful verdicts about others without checking them. You were listening when we uttered falsehoods about others, putting them in a bad light — yes, when we slandered them, thus depriving them of their honour and ruining their good reputation. Forgive us for having caused distress for others in this way.

Lord Jesus, we have sinned against You, for whatever we do to one of Your disciples we do to You. Shed Your light into our hearts and lives and reveal such sins to us, so that we can repent and confess them. May this be a comfort to You in Your suffering. Help us also to publicly restore the honour of those whose reputation we have damaged.   Amen.

choir

> I mourn about my sinning
> That caused You, Lord, such pain.
> It brought You grievous suff'ring;
> I sinned and sinned again.
> I'm only just beginning
> My depths of sin to see,
> And thank You for forgiving
> A sinner such as me.

I mourn that by my sinning
I caused You so much grief,
My dearest Lord and Saviour,
Who brought but joy to me.
My heart cries out, lamenting
My guilt and my disgrace.
I have but one petition:
In mercy grant me grace.

melody WJ 170

*When Pilate heard that Jesus had let Himself be called the Christ, the King of the Jews, he grew somewhat pensive. Leaving the open terrace, he entered the adjoining courtroom, and passing by, he looked intently at Jesus and ordered the guards to bring Him in.

When he saw Jesus so disfigured and piteous, it seemed even more ludicrous to him that this should be the Anointed One of God, the King. But because Jesus' enemies had presented their accusations in such a way as to insinuate that He was encroaching upon the rights of Caesar, Pilate summoned Jesus for cross-examination. And we know how he then asked Jesus, "Are you the King of the Jews?" — at which Jesus replied that He was the King of Truth.

After that Pilate called down from the terrace to the accusers, "I find no crime in this man!" This caused Jesus' enemies to fly into a new rage and they produced a torrent of accusations against Him. But our Lord Jesus stood there in silence and prayed for His enemies.

And when Pilate asked Jesus if He had nothing to say to all these accusations, He answered not a word, although at a Roman court one could defend oneself and thus possibly prolong the trial.

The witnesses continued their angry tirades and stated how Jesus had spread His teaching throughout Galilee.

Pilate, unable to reach a decision, clutched at this remark in his uncertainty and said, "Since he is a Galilean and a subject of Herod, take him to Herod. He is here at the feast; he can judge him."

Accordingly, Pilate sent Jesus down to the courtyard again, to His enemies. At the same time he sent an officer to Herod with the message that he was sending him one of his subjects, a Galilean, Jesus of Nazareth, to be tried. Pilate was glad that he could disentangle himself in this way and avoid sentencing Jesus, for the whole affair seemed uncanny to him. At the same time it was a political move, for he and Herod had been at enmity; and now he wished to use the opportunity to pay a courtesy to Herod, who had always been curious to see Jesus.

Jesus' enemies, infuriated at being dismissed by Pilate before all the people and at the case being remitted to Herod, vented their rage on Jesus. Together with their court servants, they surrounded Him and set Him in chains again. Pushing and beating Him, they drove Him through the crowds in the forum in wild haste and then down the street to Herod's palace, which was not far away. Herod awaited the procession in a large hall, where he was seated upon a throne, surrounded by many of his courtiers and soldiers.

Herod felt flattered that Pilate publicly gave him the right to judge a Galilean. He was most officious and pompous in his manner. It pleased him to see Jesus so humiliated, for Jesus had always declined to appear before him. Herod stared at Him inquisitively, taking in His wretched appearance. Jesus had been maltreated and beaten; His face was covered with blood and filth, and His garment was soiled. A sickening feeling of pity came over this effeminate and sensual king, and he commanded water to be brought, and amid further brutality Jesus was washed. His face, already cut and bruised, was wounded even more as they rubbed at it maliciously.

Herod now became very talkative, reciting to Jesus all that he knew about Him. He demanded to see one of His signs. "I adjure you to perform one of your miracles. You will profit by it." But Jesus did not utter a syllable in reply, and His silence maddened Herod, who felt humiliated in the sight of all those present. He poured forth a stream of questions. "Who are you? What are you about? Who gave you power? Why don't you do anything more? Are you the one about whose birth people tell strange stories? Once wise men came from the Orient ... Give account of yourself. What kind of king are you? Truly, I see nothing kingly about you. Recently a triumphal procession was held for you to the Temple, so I hear. What was the meaning of that? Tell us, how is it that it has come to such an end?" Herod asked many more such questions, but Jesus remained silent.*

choir

Jesus was silent; He opened not His mouth.

*Then Herod was told that Jesus had called him a fox and that He was working to bring about the downfall of his family. At this Herod heaped scorn and insults upon Jesus, and addressing his bodyguard and servants (he must have had a few hundred of them in his palace), he said, "Take him out. Give this ludicrous king the honour he deserves. He is more of a fool than a criminal!"

Accordingly, our Lord Jesus was led into a large courtyard, where He was most cruelly derided. They clad Him in a large sack, which reached down over His feet, and a white cloak was thrown over Him. Seeking to render a service to Herod, the soldiers and attendants did obeisance to Jesus, pushed Him to and fro, swore at Him, spat at Him and pretended to show Him all manner of royal honours. At each act they burst out in raucous laughter, jeers and taunts. In this way they maltreated Jesus and insulted Him as a mock king.*

all sing

> I've seen a wondrous picture
> That shines in heav'n above.
> The Lamb of God in suff'ring —
> The portrait of His love.
> 'Tis God Himself in torment,
> In pain and agony.
> The Lamb blasphemed and beaten
> Goes forth to Calvary.
>
> I've seen a wondrous picture
> That shines resplendently.
> 'Tis Christ, despised, yet glorious
> In all His suffering.
> Such beauty earth and heaven
> Have never seen before.
> On bended knee His ransomed
> Eternally adore.

melody WJ 62 or
"The Church's One Foundation"

Jesus, the King, is mocked by Herod! Are we not struck by the fact that here too — as at all the other trials — the main dispute is about Jesus' kingship? When Jesus is cross-examined by the Sanhedrin, He is asked whether He is the King, the Messiah, and Pilate's first question is "Are you a king?" In each instance the point in question is Jesus' kingship — no doubt because Jesus truly is the King of kings.

Indeed, Jesus testified to His accusers that He was the King of Truth. He had already proved Himself as a King of might, a King whom wind and waves had to obey, who possessed power over death. He had demonstrated His royal authority by giving ordinances — the commandments of the Sermon on the Mount, which were commandments of love. All the questions, problems and social needs of a nation would be solved, if people would live according to these commandments in the power of Jesus' redemption. The true King had come indeed. Jerusalem had seen her King entering her gates on Palm Sunday.

But what have we sons of men, who are the work of His hands, done with our King? What did His people do with Him? He had come as King first and foremost for them. He had entered His city, Jerusalem, the city of the King. There He should have ascended the throne. From there His royal dominion should have spread abroad. From there His commandments, summed up in the Sermon on the Mount, should have been proclaimed. His law of love was supposed to be applied first among His chosen people and then go forth into all the world.

What a tremendous moment it was for Jerusalem, the royal city, when at last the King of heaven entered her gates!

How His people had longed for their King, for the great Ruler, the Messiah, and for proofs of His power! But when He did come, they did not want Him! Instead they cast Him out of the city and had Him crucified. Whether it was the High Priests and the Pharisees, the representatives of the devout, or whether it was Herod and Pilate — they all wanted a king who would not infringe on their rights or make demands that would interfere with their lives. And yet was it not the religious people who seemed to have the greatest desire for the

Messiah? They continually searched the Scriptures to ascertain when He would come, and prayed ardently for His coming. But now that He had come, they sentenced Him to death. And why? Because they were envious. They could not bear to have anyone acknowledged as greater than themselves and recognized as Lord by the people.

Yet Pilate and Herod, the chief priests and elders were not the only ones to reject Jesus. The entire populace no longer wanted Jesus as King as soon as they felt that it would cost them too much to confess their loyalty to this King. No one wanted Him! No, not one!

These events must cut us to the quick, because this attitude is typical of all humanity. None of us wants to accept Jesus as King. We all want to create our own king. We want to have a king whom we can rule according to our own will, whom we can treat as we please. On the one hand, we long for Jesus as King. We yearn to experience His love, His help, His miracles. But ultimately we do not wish to recognize Him as Lord and King if He shows us the truth as He did Herod. We are too proud. We reject Him when He comes as Judge, when He humbles and judges us for the sins that we tolerate in our lives.

Because everyone wants to be his own king, his own lord, the shout has gone up today that man must be autonomous, free to rule and make his own decisions. But man, enslaved by sin and Satan, fails miserably in all his attempts to rule by himself.

There is only one true Lord and King, and this is Jesus Christ. There has never been a king like Him, nor will there ever be. Endowed with nobility and splendour, glory and majesty, He is the King of kings and Lord of lords. He is the King of truth, of righteousness and love, who can bring righteousness, prosperity and true happiness to the nations, because He alone has the power to set us free from the chains of our sins and to remould us into new men who in turn can form a new world.

Yet nowadays, as in times of old, no one wants Jesus as King! Thus to this very day Jerusalem, the royal city, has neither a royal residence nor a throne. She does not yet have her King, although in Scripture she is called "the city of the great King" (Psalm 48). And likewise mankind does not yet have its King — to this day He has not been able to establish His kingdom of peace and righteousness.

Today Jesus' honour is being dragged in the dust as never before; His majesty and kingly dignity as the Lord of lords is being profaned. Like Herod long ago, man once more dares to blaspheme Jesus, the King, portraying Him as a clown, while homage is paid to autonomous man.

> The world denies the King of kings
> The honour that is His.
> Lament, proclaim and sing aloud;
> Declare who Jesus is!

choir

> Jesus, O Jesus, King of great glory,
> Endowed with splendour and majesty.
> Jesus, Jesus, I worship You.

> Jesus, exalted, filled with God's glory,
> O Son of God, all praise be to You!
> Jesus, Jesus, I worship You.

> Jesus, our King, majestic and splendid,
> Soon all the worlds will lie at Your feet.
> Jesus, Jesus, I worship You.[1]

[1] *Glory Be to God* ("Praise Be to Jesus", verses 1, 10, 31)

Today Jesus is waiting for His little flock, the bride of the Lamb, to honour Him as King by portraying a kingdom of love, where they live according to His commandments and submit unconditionally to His rule, His will and leadings.

Then there will be a foreshadowing of Jesus' dominion where He will be able to truly reign as King over His little flock. This would be a sign that the day will soon come when the bride of the Lamb will be completed and perfected, and when the shout of jubilation will resound through the air, "The kingdom of the world has become the kingdom of our Lord and of his Christ." Then when Jesus vanquishes the Antichrist with the breath of His mouth, He will take over all the kingdoms of this world and be recognized as King by mankind, whom He created.

Let us pray together.

all pray

Lord Jesus,

We cannot stand by and watch while You, the one true King, are held up to contempt and ridicule and so blasphemed. How it grieves us that to this day You are unable to reveal Yourself to the world as the true King!

We want to stand at Your side even if it costs us our reputation, position, freedom, yes, our very lives to testify before men that You are the King of kings and Lord of lords.

How it grieves us that this degradation was the last impression people had of You on earth and that once more You are being shown in the image of disgrace to all! We cannot bear to see that the world continues to humiliate You deeply and make You look ridiculous, and that more than two thirds of mankind today revolt and fight against You, the King of kings, in passionate hatred.

O Lord Jesus, how it grieves us that Your people did not accept You as King! We humble ourselves that the world continues to reject Your royal dominion and Your royal ordinances, expressed in Your commandments, which ought to be binding for all humanity.

How it grieves us that because of our rebelliousness You are still unable to see the fulfilment of Your great longing, to bring us Your kingdom, as the fruit of Your bitter suffering and death, and to establish the much-desired kingdom of peace, love and righteousness!

Lord Jesus, we want to live for the dawning of Your dominion in our midst today. Accept our dedication. May our lives be a testimony that You are King and we are Your subjects, who obey You implicitly in voluntary love. May nothing be left of our rights and claims, or our desire for recognition and honour. We do not wish to follow our own wills or live for the fulfilment of our personal desires, but rather take Your will as binding for us.

O Lord Jesus Christ, in the power of Your blood we have been redeemed from the desire to rule our own lives. We wish to consent to all that You ordain for us, even when our will is frustrated and our pride rebels against Your leading.

May our consent help to pave the way for You to come as King. We pray that others may ask about our King when they see that a life lived under Your dominion and based on Your commandments is the solution to all problems and the source of true happiness and well-being.

Amen.

JESUS ON TRIAL BEFORE PILATE'S SUPREME COURT

all sing

Dearest Jesus, who can measure
All the pain that You endured —
Slander, scorn, spit, blows and fetters —
Son of God, so righteous, pure,
Satan's bonds of sin to sever,
From his pow'r my soul deliver!
Thousand, thousand thanks be Yours,
Dearest Jesus, evermore.

How You let Yourself be wounded,
Cruelly treated and abased,
To relieve my soul's affliction
And to save me by Your grace!
You endured such evil cursing,
That I might obtain God's blessing!
Thousand, thousand thanks be Yours,
Dearest Jesus, evermore.

Oh, how cruelly man has mocked You,
Treating You with shame and scorn!
Lord, what made You bear such insults,
Even to be crowned with thorns?
That I might have joy for ever
And be crowned above with honour!
Thousand, thousand thanks be Yours,
Dearest Jesus, evermore.

cf. EKG 65

*Desiring to please Pilate, Herod sent Jesus back with the comment that Jesus was a fool but that he had found no crime in Him.

The chief priests and the enemies of Jesus returned by a different route, one that was probably twice as long, in order to exhibit Him in His great disgrace in another part of the city. They also wanted to mistreat Him longer on the way and to leave their agitators enough time to win the crowds for their evil plans. Giving a large amount of money to some of their number, they sent them to another part of the city, where many of the Pharisees were staying, with the bidding that they gather in the vicinity of Pilate's palace together with their communities. The money was to be distributed among the people, so that they would demand Jesus' crucifixion with great vehemence and by no means plead for His release.

Others were sent to threaten the people that if they did not demand the death of this blasphemer, they would be drawing God's judgment down upon themselves. They also spread the rumour that if Jesus did not die He would join forces with the Romans and that this was the kingdom of which He had spoken.

The path along which Jesus' enemies now took Him was considerably worse and extremely rugged. They were always at His side, continually goading on the executioners that led Him. The long garment hindered our Lord as He walked. He fell to the ground several times. Raining blows upon His head and kicking Him, the executioners hauled Him back to His feet with the ropes. No words can describe the mockery and brutality with which He was treated. Jeering mobs surrounded Him, for the sneering Pharisees who led the way had stirred up the rabble everywhere. The procession now drew near Pilate's residence. As Jesus was dragged up the stairs leading to it, He tripped over His loose garment and fell so violently that drops of blood from His holy head fell upon the white marble steps.

Once more our Lord Jesus stood before Pilate. According to an old custom the people would gather there about this time of year, before the Passover, with a petition for the release of a prisoner. Pilate hoped that the people would demand Jesus' freedom and he intended to offer them the release of either Jesus or a terrible villain, who had already been condemned to death, so that they would have no alternative. This criminal was Barabbas and he was detested by all the people. He had committed the most vile abominations and practised sorcery.

When the Pharisees and the people now petitioned for a release, the Mother Mary together with others hoped and prayed that they would not commit so great a crime as to prefer the murderer to her Son. The rumour that Pilate was trying to release Jesus had also reached her ears. Not far away from her stood large numbers of people from Capernaum, many of whom Jesus had taught and healed. They stole furtive glances at the unhappy, veiled women and the disciple John, acting as if they did not know them. Mary thought that these would surely reject Barabbas in favour of Jesus, their Benefactor and Saviour. But this was not so!

After Jesus' first trial Pilate was adjured by his wife *not* to condemn Jesus, because she had been shown in a dream that this should not be. He had given her his word and shortly before Jesus appeared before him for the second time, he had even returned the pledge to her as a sign that he still intended to keep his promise and release Jesus.

Pilate stepped out again on the terrace and sat down on the throne. The chief priests had also taken their seats, and Pilate called out, "Which of these two men shall I release for you?" Across the forum and from all sides the loud cries arose, "Away with him! Give us Barabbas!" Pilate called out once more, "Then what should I do with Jesus, who is supposed to be the Christ, the King of the Jews?" A deafening clamour followed as they all cried, "Crucify him!" Pilate asked them a third time, "Why, what evil has he done? I have found in him no crime deserving death; I will therefore chastise him and release him." But the shouts of "Crucify him! Crucify him!" thundered across the forum as if a storm from hell had broken out, and the chief priests and Pharisees were almost frantic with raging and shouting.

Then the irresolute Pilate released the villain Barabbas.*

O lament! A murderer is preferred to the pure and holy Son of God!

O lament the wickedness of our hearts that prefers to let an evil man live and the pure and holy Lord be murdered on the cross!

O lament the wickedness of our hearts! By exonerating Barabbas, who is guilty, we absolve ourselves. We seek to be free and thus the innocent Lord is made a victim of death — for our sakes.

O lament what we did to Jesus here and what we inflict upon Him today in the wickedness of our hearts! Today too the pure and sinless Son of God is portrayed to the world as a criminal.

O lament! Robbers, criminals and murderers are honoured by men today also, whereas the innocent are condemned unjustly.

O lament! All the wickedness and vulgarity in our hearts and lives is attributed to Him — and His own do not speak out.

O lament that this could happen long ago and once again today! It will be a reproach to us for all eternity. We are the ones, the Christians, who in our desire to please others or in fear of causing offence remain silent when such great injustice is committed against Jesus. In doing so, we deliver up Jesus anew into the hands of His enemies.

choir

> O mourn and lament throughout the lands!
> Lament o'er the fathomless grief of God
> That Jesus is blasphemed, forsaken!
> God's heart is breaking with anguish great,
> Is grieved unto death as in Noah's day.
> O come ye and join my lamenting!
> Lament! God is grieving, is grieving.
> O weep, O weep, lament and mourn
> Over the sins of the world.
> O who is prepared to stand now by Jesus,
>   the Saviour,
> To suffer for Him today?

Let us humbly confess together:

all pray

We are the ones, Lord Jesus, who, wavering like Pilate, betray You for the sake of our prestige, popularity and reputation. We are irresolute and easily swayed by others. Although we know who You are, we do not take our stand beside You when there is a price to be paid. At the same time, like Pilate, we hypocritically pride ourselves on being just, unbiased and neutral. In Your immeasurable suffering You show us the dreadful consequences of our attitude and our desire not to incur anyone's displeasure.

Lord, hear our prayer and in the power of Your bitter suffering deliver us from this serious bondage to sin, so that we do not betray You the moment our testimony to You will cost us much. We beseech You, prepare us now and help us to fight against all fear of men, desire to win their favour, and dependency on their opinions, all weakness of character, pliability and cowardice. Help us to fight this battle even to the point of shedding blood, so that we do not become Your enemies and tormentors in the time of persecution, in the hour of testing. Strengthen us to walk the path of suffering with You as Your true disciples, and grant that one day we may inherit the crown of life.

Amen.

all sing

> Grant that we too may brave
> The battle and affliction,
> Not losing heart beneath
> Our cross' heavy burden.
> Grant us the strength with which
> You bore the crown of thorns,
> That we may patiently
> Face death, disgrace and scorn.

cf. EKG 66
can be sung to the melody,
"Now Thank We All Our God"

JESUS IS SCOURGED

all sing

> Heaven bows itself in wonder;
> Angels, awestruck, veil their sight!
> Weep, O heavens, don your mourning;
> Darkened be your rays of light!
> God's own Son is bound for scourging,
> Stripped and naked, to the post,
> There the cruel stripes awaiting
> On the way to shameful death.

melody WJ 64 or "Love
Divine, All Loves Excelling"

*Pilate, that low-minded, irresolute judge, publicly uttered the contradictory, nonsensical words, "I have found no crime in him; I will therefore chastise him and release him." He gave the order for Jesus to be scourged in Roman style, although he knew that scourging often resulted in death. Thereupon, the court servants with pushes and blows led Jesus, our Saviour, who had been mistreated and spat upon, through the raging, clamorous crowd to the whipping post.

Four executioners now came with their whips, rods and ropes, which they threw down at the foot of the pillar. They approached Jesus — uncouth criminals who worked as slaves and convicts on building sites and canals. The most wicked and unscrupulous of them were selected for such tasks as scourging in the praetorium. The men, who were half-drunk, had something fiendish about them. They struck our Lord with clenched fists and ropes and in a frenzy they dragged Him to the whipping post, although He was so willing to go. No words can describe the barbarous treatment that Jesus suffered at the hands of these frenzied executioners during this short stretch to the pillar.

Tearing off the cloak that they had put on Him at the trial before Herod, they almost knocked the Son of God down to the ground. With His hands swollen and bleeding from the ropes, Jesus quickly took off His clothes by Himself, while the executioners jostled Him. All this time Jesus prayed and entreated the Father. He now embraced the pillar. It was so high that a tall man would have had to stretch his arms to reach the iron ring fastened at the top. Rings and hooks were attached to the other side of the pillar as well. The executioners, cursing abominably, stretched Jesus' arms, tied His hands to the iron ring at the top and raised His body so high that His feet, which were fastened at the foot of the pillar, scarcely touched the ground. Exposed to the utmost shame, the only-begotten Son of God stood bound to the post, a place fit only for a criminal.

Two of the bloodthirsty villains began in a rage to lash His holy back, covering it entirely with wounds. Our Lord and Saviour, very God and very man, winced and writhed like a worm beneath the strokes of the criminals.*

all sing

> I caused You such affliction,
> O Jesus, my Salvation.
> I wrought Your misery.
> O Lord, we and our offspring
> Have sinned from the beginning;
> Yet You have never sinned at all!

cf. EKG 64

Yes, we are the ones who have struck Jesus with our words and actions when we were annoyed or angry. Ultimately it is Jesus who is made to suffer the consequences of our lashing out. The scourging is an appalling illustration that ever since the Fall we men, who were actually created in the image of God, have a strong, evil, satanic impulse to beat and torment others. Six million Jews were killed by us Germans, and over 90 million people have been put to death in atheistic countries. All the countless blows ever dealt by man have fallen upon Jesus — including ours. Jesus suffered the scourging once long ago and suffers it today anew when millions give vent to their rage in destructiveness and violence. And even if we have not taken part in such acts, must we not ask ourselves as Christians, "Have we lashed out at others in our reproachful thoughts and words, criticizing them or condemning them by what we say or by the way we act? And when anger got the better of us, have we sometimes actually struck them?"

Jesus bore all these blows and continues to do so, also suffering them with the many innocent ones who undergo such treatment. Jesus bears these blows as no one could ever bear them — with infinite humility and immeasurable love as the Lamb of God, who was always found patient.

For the sake of Jesus' suffering at the whipping post, let us now renounce all our vehemence and anger, which can lead to real blows, torment and murder. Let us renounce our determination to have our own way, our irritability, our faultfinding, our anger and hatred. These sins are the cause of many crimes now at the dawn of the anti-Christian era, when no day passes by without assaults and even sadistic murders being committed.

(short pause for silent prayer)

I pray that in Your name, Jesus, these demonic powers, which provoke me to lose my temper, to act in anger, malice and rebellion will depart from me. I praise You for having redeemed me from such sinful behaviour and actions. And I renounce this disposition, which stems from the devil himself.

Lord, perform a miracle in me, I pray, through the creative power of the Holy Spirit, so that every time I am on the verge of losing my temper and lashing out in annoyance and anger, I must restrain myself, being reminded of You standing at the whipping post. Let me be convicted by Your image, O Lamb that bore all these inhuman lashes so quietly and submissively for us.

If one day the hour should come for me to be beaten, help me, my Lord Jesus, to stand at Your side. Prepare me especially for the time of persecution when we shall be cruelly beaten and tormented. Prepare me for the sake of Your holy blood that flowed for me at the whipping post. Make me meek and humble, that I can endure the torment silently without rebelling and that I can reflect Your image, O Lamb of God.

Even now I surrender myself in spirit ever anew to all this suffering with the words of love, "For You, Lord Jesus, for You!"

My Lord Jesus, I trust that when the time comes You will grant me Your spirit of meekness, demonstrate Your power in my weakness, and bring me through, never letting me be tempted beyond my strength.

I shall follow You in affliction and even unto death. Help me to keep this promise. Jesus, I want to follow You as Your little lamb and suffer for You in the time of persecution in love and gratitude for Your agonizing scourging, Your bitter suffering and death."

Amen.

O Man of Sorrows wounded sore,
My love to Thee belongeth.
Thy body with its thousand wounds
Thy love for me proclaimeth.

O Man of Sorrows, Thee I love.
Thou showest forth love only,
Which God imprinteth on Thy face —
In pain endowed with beauty.

For Thee alone I yearn to live,
O my belovèd Saviour.
With all my heart at one with Thee,
In meekness I would suffer.

can be sung to the melody, "The King of Love My Shepherd Is"

*Jesus sighed and moaned in heart-rending agony, His high-pitched cries of lamentation rising like a loving prayer above the swish of the lashes cast by His tormentors. From time to time these painful tones of lament and blessing were drowned by the shouts of the people and the Pharisees, which were like the rumbling of a terrible, black storm cloud. Once more the crowds began to shout, "Crucify him!", for Pilate continued to negotiate with them. When he wished to interrupt the tumult of the crowd with a few words, a trumpet was blown to command silence. Then once again the sound of the lashes, Jesus' plaintive cries and the curses of the executioners could be heard — but also the bleating of the paschal lambs, which were being washed east of the praetorium in the sheep pond near the Sheep Gate. It was heart-moving to hear the bleating of the helpless lambs, for theirs were the only voices that blended with the sighs of our Saviour.

In accordance with their law the Jewish people kept their distance from the whipping post, about the width of a street. Only the width of a street! There they stood as spectators — and jeered!

Jesus' body was brown and blue and red, covered with weals. Blood was trickling down from His wounds. He trembled and winced. Taunts and jeers sounded on all sides.

After a quarter of an hour the first pair of executioners was relieved by a second pair, who fell upon Jesus savagely. They applied a different type of rod studded with thorns and barbed hooks. At their frenzied lashing all the weals on Jesus' holy body were ripped open.*

choir

> Thy back was deeply furrowed,
> O dearest Lamb Divine.
> O who can ever measure
> The torture that was Thine!
> Thy wounds were bleeding freely
> As savage whips attacked.
> And, Jesus, still our lashes
> Rain blows upon Thy back.

melody WJ 62

Who can comprehend Jesus' immeasurable heartache today? After having submitted to the cruel lashes of the scourging because of our sinful desires, He now has to experience that even Christians, though knowing of His Passion, disrespect His commandments and indulge in the sins of the flesh, including fornication. In doing so, they are guilty of scourging and beating Jesus anew.

How the angelic choirs must fill the heavens with their strains of lament! Had not the angels, full of grief, once seen their Lord cruelly scourged for the sake of the sons of men and their sins? But today the angels are witnessing how Jesus must suffer anew because of human lust — a sin that even Christians indulge in.

Today the hate-filled opponents of Jesus attribute their sins to Him, the pure and spotless Son of God, branding Him as one of their own kind, as a sensualist without any inhibitions, who gave free rein to his drives.

Thus He is presented in a fiendish, degrading manner to mankind in publications, film and stage productions. This is the most flagrant form of blasphemy. How serious, therefore, is every sin of self-indulgence! For we are to blame that these sins are now attributed to Jesus. It is for our sins that He must once more suffer such agony.

all speak

> Forgive me, Lord, forgive my sins, I pray,
> For they have caused You agony today.
> I lie before You, weeping o'er my guilt.
> 'Tis I, O Lord, 'tis I that am to blame
> That You are seen by man in such deep shame.
> My Jesus, hear my prayer, forgive my sins.

speaker

> The heart of God is bleeding,
> Filled with anguish deep,
> Wounded by His children —
> Oh, who can plumb His grief?
> Men rob Him of His honour,
> Despise His majesty
> And tread His glory in the dust.
> O untold agony!

The angel hosts are weeping
That those whom God created
Should dare attack their Lord,
Who is their Maker, God.
And Jesus, humbled to the dust,
Is filled with suffering,
For none today believes
That He is Lord and Saviour,
That He alone is King.

Deprived of all His honour,
Disfigured and disgraced,
Portrayed by man as though enslaved to sin,
He is despised and hated —
Our Lord, who is pure Love.
Oh, who can fathom such iniquity as this!

The Holy One is standing
Disgraced before all lands.
Man's wickedness holds sway.
And Jesus? Silently He waits,
Humbly, till the day when He
Will be revealed to all as God,
The living God, who judges sin.

*Finally the executioners ceased their thrashing and Jesus, as if in a faint, sank down at the foot of the whipping post in a pool of blood, His body so cruelly disfigured. The executioners took a drink and called out to the soldiers, who were busy in the guardhouse, telling them to weave the crown of thorns.

Throughout the scourging as the strokes rained down upon Him, causing Him dreadful agony, Jesus surrendered Himself continually to the Father for the sins of mankind. But now as Jesus lay in His blood at the foot of the post, an angel strengthened Him.

Then the executioners returned. They pushed Him with their feet and ordered Him to stand up, saying that they were not yet finished with the "king". The villains laughed scornfully and kicked Him back and forth, so that Jesus painfully writhed on the ground like a worm trodden under foot.*

Here Jesus had to suffer the fulfilment of the prophetic words in the Psalm of suffering, "I am a worm and no man; scorned by men, and despised by the people" (Psalm 22: 6).

God Himself, the second Person of the Godhead, writhes in His own blood like a worm, naked because of our shamelessness. Jesus' wounds are bleeding because of our carnal sins, our sensualism and the other desires of our lower nature, which manifest themselves in many different ways.

How dearly Jesus had to pay for all these sins! Let us never forget the image of Jesus writhing like a worm at the whipping post, a spectacle for the people! The Son of God took upon Himself human form and offered up His body to such inhuman treatment that it was disfigured almost beyond recognition. The sins of sensuality are so terrible that nothing less than the cruel torture of His holy body could pay for them.

all pray

We humble ourselves before You, O Lamb of God, so disfigured and tormented. Oh, may we lie before You in the dust, O Saviour, scourged for our sakes. For You bore the horrible leprosy of our sin, atoned for our iniquity and suffered our punishment. We are the cause of Your immeasurable torment at the whipping post. Forgive us all our impurity and unchastity. Forgive us for whenever we have yielded to the desires of the flesh — our inordinate desire for food or sleep, our evil fantasy. For all this You had to pay the penalty. With Your pure and holy blood cover each one of these sins that we have ever committed. We want to confess them and break with them, so that we do not come under judgment one day — the judgment that awaits adulterers and harlots.

Because of our carnal sins You suffered heart-rending pain, inhuman disgrace and torment as the holy Lamb of God at the whipping post. O Jesus, we thank and worship You for this.

During Your immeasurable torment and humiliation You continued to love us, Your children, who are covered with filth. O Jesus, we are for ever grateful to You.

Your wounds are our salvation. Now our sinful bodies, defiled by the sins of the flesh, can become whole again, and instead of rising to disgrace in eternity and bearing sickness and pain for ever, we may receive a body of divine beauty. Jesus, we worship You for this.

O Jesus, Lamb of God, our Saviour, scourged for our sakes, we shall thank You for ever and ever. And we shall bless You without end that we may bear a spotless and pure, glorious and radiant resurrection body for all eternity if we overcome in the struggle against the sins of the flesh in the power of Your blood.

                                          Amen.

choir

> O come, bewail in sorrow
> The scourging of our Lord
> Till all the world does wonder,
> "Who is so praised, adored?"
> Till earth and heaven marvel
> How loved our Lord must be,
> And man, repenting, worships
> The Lamb on bended knee.

JESUS CROWNED WITH THORNS

all sing

> I thank You, Lord, You gaze so tenderly
> Beneath the thorns — imprint this sight on me.
>
> I thank You, Lord, such mockery You bear,
> That I one day a glorious crown may wear.
>
> I thank You, Lord, You bear the crown of thorn;
> May glory Your humility adorn.

melody WJ 93

*While Jesus was being scourged, Pilate spoke with the people several times, during which one of them cried out, "He must go, even if it means death for us all!" And when Jesus was led away to be crowned with thorns, they continued to cry, "Away with him, away with him!" The messengers sent out by the chief priests had gathered more and more people and incited them to join in the clamour.

Jesus was now led into the inner courtyard of the guardhouse to be mocked and crowned with thorns. About fifty executioners and slaves, unscrupulous ruffians, took an active part in ill-treating Jesus here. At the beginning the crowd surged forward, but then hundreds of Roman soldiers surrounded the building. They stood in formation, laughing and scoffing and thus inciting Jesus' tormentors to even greater brutalities, for the latter responded to the laughter and jests as actors would to applause.*

It is almost incomprehensible that Jesus could endure more suffering and still survive. Supernatural strength must have been imparted to Him. Angels may have come to strengthen Him, so that He could bear even more suffering. Jesus was now led to be crowned with thorns — half-dead and yet unable to die, since He had to complete the full measure of suffering and atone for the sin of all mankind.

*His tormentors had rolled the pedestal of an old pillar into the middle of the courtyard. On top of it they placed a low footstool, which they maliciously covered with sharp stones and fragments of pottery. Once again they tore all the clothing off Jesus' wounded body and placed upon Him a tattered, red soldier's coat that did not even reach His knees.

They now dragged Jesus to the seat covered with broken pottery and sharp stones. Then they set the crown of thorns upon Him, placing it like a bandeau round His forehead and tying it together at the back. The sturdy thorn branches were woven together by hand with most of the thorns intentionally pointed inward. Next they placed in Jesus' hand a thick reed ending in a tuft. All this they did with mock ceremony as though they were really crowning Him king. They took the reed out of His hand and vehemently struck the crown with it. Blood filled the eyes of Jesus. They knelt down before Him, stuck their tongues out at Him, struck Him and spat in His face and shouted, "Hail, King of the Jews!"

Jesus suffered terrible thirst. The lacerations of the inhuman scourging had given Him wound-fever. He trembled. His flesh was torn in places down to His very ribs. His tongue stuck to the roof of His mouth and only His holy blood that flowed down from His head took mercy upon His burning lips. For about half an hour Jesus was subjected to the cruel treatment, and the cohort that stood in formation round the praetorium laughed and shouted their approval.*

Jesus is the pure and innocent Lamb of God who did only good to all. It is incomprehensible that man dared to torment Him with this diabolical laughter and scorn and derision. But far more incomprehensible was Jesus' response. Lovingly He looked upon His tormentors with a mild, forgiving expression on His sorely bruised countenance beneath the crown of thorns.

> His countenance is shining,
> Gentle in deepest suff'ring
> Beneath the crown of thorns.
> 'Tis stronger than the scoffing,
> Has power for atoning,
> For blotting out each sin and curse.

all pray

Lord Jesus,

Imprint deeply upon our hearts Your wounded, blood-stained countenance beneath the crown of thorns. Though in deepest agony, You gazed upon Your tormentors so mildly. Let us keep this image before our eyes when people hurt, slander or wrong us. We are ashamed that as sinners, who have deserved such treatment, we dare to take offence or feel bitter. Lord Jesus, we do not wish to increase Your torment with our sinful reactions when we are hurt by others, for our suffering is so small and it is our due reward. We yearn to be so transformed that when we are insulted today and persecuted tomorrow we may react like You, bearing our enemies in love and responding to insults with mercy as You have borne us in love and mercy. In this way we want to thank You for Your immeasurable suffering when You were crowned with thorns. Please grant us this love for the sake of Your outpoured blood.

Amen.

*Jesus was now led by the soldiers back into Pilate's palace, the crown of thorns upon His head, the reed as a sceptre in His bound hands, the purple cloak draped round His shoulders. Our Lord was unrecognizable because of the blood that filled His eyes and trickled down into His mouth and beard. His body was covered with weals and wounds. He walked bent over with faltering steps. His cloak was so short that He had to stoop in order to conceal His nakedness, for they had torn off all His clothing again when they crowned Him with thorns. As Jesus was brought before Pilate, a feeling of pity mingled with disgust ran through even this cruel man.

After Jesus was painfully dragged up the steps, He was placed in the background, while Pilate stepped forward on the terrace. A trumpet was blown in order to gain the attention of the people, for Pilate wished to speak. He addressed the chief priests and all who were present, saying, "Behold, I am bringing him out to you once more, that you may know that I find no crime in him."

Jesus was now brought forward by the soldiers and placed next to Pilate on the terrace, so that all the people in the forum could see Him. Jesus stood there before Pilate's palace in His purple cloak — His body lacerated, His face covered with blood, His bowed head pierced by thorns, His bound hands holding the reed as a sceptre. He stood there in immeasurable gentleness and sadness, filled with grief and love. It was a terrible, heart-rending sight, which at first evoked dread and a stunned silence, as the Son of God, mistreated and blood-stained, bearing the terrible crown of thorns, turned His eyes upon the surging crowds. Pilate stepped beside Him, pointed at Him and called down to the Jews, "Behold, here is the man!"*

O sight demanding silence!
In heav'n all bow to rev'rence
The Lamb with crown of thorns.
Adoring angels, gazing
Upon this sight amazing,
Perplexed, can never understand.

O pain beyond conceiving,
Lamenting angels grieving
Around their Maker, Lord.
Scarcely a man He stands there!
How can we God discern here
Beneath the shameful crown of thorns?

WJ 65

all sing

O sacred head, surrounded
By crown of piercing thorn!
O bleeding head, so wounded,
So shamed and put to scorn!
O sacred head, once glorious
With highest majesty,
How pale Thy face with anguish,
Now scorned so bitterly!

O countenance so noble,
Before which everyone
Should stand in awe and tremble,
Now pale and spat upon!
Thine eyes once shone with beauty,
With matchless light and grace!
Who treated Thee so cruelly
And caused Thee such disgrace?

cf. EKG 63

We lament that Your countenance, the most beautiful of all countenances, was disfigured, torn open and covered with blood beneath the crown of thorns. It was rendered unrecognizable because of our sins — our vanity and our craving for attention, honour and prestige.

We lament that Your countenance of sublime holiness and beauty, in which the heavens were reflected, upon which all the hosts of cherubim gazed in adoration and in whose radiance mankind found healing, is now disfigured, its radiance gone.

Oh, Lord Jesus, we can see our sin in Your disfigured human countenance, so filled with grief.

Today we see millions of young people with disfigured faces, distorted by sins and addictions, although You have redeemed them to bear Your image. What immeasurable grief the sight of them must now bring to Your heart! You bore this disfigured, distorted and ugliest of all human faces, so that there no longer need be a disfigured human face. And we shall reflect Your image if we behold Your countenance of eternal majesty beneath the crown of thorns and let Your traits be imprinted upon us, thanking You for Your redemption and giving You our love.

We want to dedicate ourselves to You and say:

all pray

Our Lord Jesus,

Long ago and once again today disgrace and shame are heaped upon You. Let us stand at Your side. In our personal lives now and later during persecution, when we are despised, slandered, shunned and persecuted for the sake of Your name, we want to stand by You, our Lord crowned with thorns.

Prepare us to bear all this quietly and out of love for You, following Your example and the example of Your apostles and witnesses. Make us willing to become a spectacle before the visible and invisible world, to be held up as the most despised, the least of all men, and to be subjected to the most terrible verdicts in public. Grant that we may become like You in this respect.

Yes, we pray, let us remember how You beheld Your blasphemers with mercy, so that we may reflect Your image of love and testify to Your redeeming love. Grant that through this many may come to believe in You.

We thank You that when we are suffering disgrace, especially during the time of persecution, we may look forward to the day when You will come again and we shall behold Your countenance, which shines like the sun in ineffable majesty and divine nobility. What a triumph it will be on that day when people will fall down before You and honour You as the King of kings after having mocked and despised You — once long ago when Your countenance was disfigured beneath the crown of thorns and again today! This prospect is our consolation in view of Your immeasurable suffering.

Amen.

(Let us have a few moments of quiet for making a committal to bear disgrace and disfigurement for Jesus' sake, praying in faith that He will then lay His radiance upon our faces.)

choir

> Unto You alone, my Saviour,
> I would look when I must suffer,
> And behold Your countenance.
> Taking in Your traits and visage,
> My heart drinks its fill, O Jesus,
> And all horrors fade away.
>
> To behold You, Lord, derided,
> Crowned with thorns and so tormented,
> Gives me strength to suffer too.

When in love You look upon me,
Darkness and despair flee from me
And Your comfort fills my soul.

When my heart is sick with sorrow,
In Your piercèd hands, my Saviour,
I shall rest and there be healed.
Jesus, I will bear wounds gladly
When Your enemies attack me.
You are worth all suffering!

all speak

When I am insulted and derided,
Laden with disgrace and ridicule,
Let me behold You in my heart, O Lord.
As Your lamb I would ever go with You.
You will impart the strength I need.

I will suffer patiently with You,
Not contend with those who torment me.
For this, O Lord, Your holy blood was shed;
It will heal my sin-sick heart and soul
And fill me with the Lamb's own patient love.

Text: John 19: 6—16

THE CONDEMNATION

*"Behold the man" — with these words the Man of
Sorrows was presented to the crowd. But the chief
priests and the officers only grew more enraged when
they saw Jesus crowned with thorns. Their consciences
were stricken at the terrible sight, for in it they could see

the reflection of their guilt. Thus they cried out again, "Away with him! Crucify him!" But Pilate called out, "Aren't you satisfied yet? He has been handled so roughly that he won't want to be a king any more!" They became almost frantic with rage, shouting even more vehemently, while the crowd cried in fury, "Away with him! To the cross with him!"

Pilate, however, was still hoping to release Jesus in some way or other. He had become unsure — partly because of his own confused thoughts, partly because of his wife's dreams, but also because of Jesus Himself and His words about the truth. Therefore, he went out on the terrace and declared once more that he intended to release Jesus. At this they all cried out, "If you release this man, you are not Caesar's friend; every one who makes himself a king sets himself against Caesar." Others threatened to complain to Caesar, saying that Jesus had been disturbing their feast. They demanded that Pilate continue with the trial, because time was short; at ten o'clock they were due in the Temple. "To the cross with him! Away with him!" The cries arose on all sides, and people were even shouting down from the flat roofs.

Pilate saw that he could achieve nothing in this tumult. There was something frightening about the raging and shouting, and the heaving mass of people in front of the palace gave every sign of developing into a major riot. He called for some water and in the sight of the people a servant poured it over his hands. Then Pilate called down from the terrace, "I am innocent of this righteous man's blood; see to it yourselves." Whereupon there arose a horrifying chanting from the assembled crowd, which had come together from all parts of the land. With one voice they cried, "His blood be on us and on our children!" Upon their threat to denounce him to Caesar, Pilate yielded to their will, thus breaking the

111

promise that he had given his wife and acting against law and justice and against his own convictions. Out of fear of Caesar, Pilate complied with their demand.*

It is incomprehensible! Out of fear of men alone, out of fear of what they may think, say or do, people deliver up Jesus, the Son of God, our Saviour, the sole Redeemer of the world — long ago and today. As Germans we abandoned the Jews to their fate during the Hitler era out of fear of men. And in doing so, we delivered up God, for the Jews are the apple of God's eye, and whatever we do to them, we do to Him. Out of fear of being mocked and of losing their reputation and perhaps their position, out of fear of being persecuted later, thousands in our churches today are keeping silent when they should be raising their voices. They tolerate it when Jesus is blasphemed, when His cross is derided; they tolerate the fact that theologians declare Him dead, that magazines blame Him for all the misery in the world, and that He is humiliated in the most degrading manner and portrayed as a clown in stage and film productions.

Long ago when Pilate pronounced the death sentence upon Jesus out of fear of men, he had nothing for his conscience but water, which could not cleanse him of his terrible guilt. We too have no excuse — not in the sight of man and by no means in the sight of God — when we deliver up Jesus to save ourselves.

Like Pilate, like the chosen people, none of us wants to be the guilty one. It is the others, so we think, or the unfavourable, difficult circumstances that are at fault. Thus we justify ourselves day by day whenever we are reproached and the blame is laid on us. But what we do not realize is that when we justify ourselves, we are condemned by God and take our place with Pilate, for Jesus' blood only pleads mercy for those who confess their guilt before God and man by admitting, "I am the one! I have sinned against heaven and before You!" May this now make us detest all self-righteousness, self-justification and self-excusing, which will bring His judgment down upon us. Let us tremble when we think of the fate of His chosen people. Under the influence of their leaders, they shouted, "Away with him!" and then for two thousand years they experienced that God really did turn away from them, because they had not accepted Jesus' blood that was shed for their sins — although ultimately God in His faithfulness did not abandon His chosen people.

As we contemplate the sufferings of Jesus, let us bear in mind that a serious judgment will come upon us if we who know so much of His suffering and redemption are so fearful of men that we fail to confess our allegiance to Him, the Son of God, our Saviour — simply because we are afraid of the suffering that such a testimony will cost us, especially in the coming time of persecution.

Therefore, we pray, Lord Jesus, be gracious to us and never let this happen. Help us now to overcome all dread of suffering and all fear of men in the power of Your blood.

*Unwilling to admit his cowardice, Pilate justified himself for pronouncing the verdict. He ascribed his decision to the dreadful shouting of the mob, thus placing the blame upon the Jews. Accordingly, he commanded everything to be prepared for the official verdict to be pronounced. He had his ceremonial robes brought out and these were placed on him. Then leaving the palace, he proceeded to the forum where, opposite the site of the scourging, there was a raised platform with the judgment seat. Verdicts were only valid when they were pronounced from here. Many soldiers surrounded the terrace.

Annas and Caiaphas and others immediately went to the judgment seat in the forum while Pilate donned his ceremonial robes. The two thieves had already been led there. And now Jesus, still wearing the tattered cloak and the crown of thorns on His head and with His hands bound, was led by the court servants and soldiers through the jeering crowd to the judgment seat and placed between the two thieves.

Jesus stood there at the foot of the steps before Pilate, surrounded by executioners; His enemies looked upon Him with malice and laughed derisively. A trumpet blew to command silence and Pilate pronounced the death sentence upon our Saviour.*

choir

> Jesus, universal Sovereign,
> He whose kingdom has no end,
> He whose splendour fills the heavens,
> Came to earth to dwell with men,
> Not to rule like earthly monarchs,
> Nor His pow'r to manifest.
> No! His heart has chosen to suffer,
> To be tried and judged for us.
>
> Come, ye angels, come, lament Him,
> Ye who stand around His throne!
> Come and raise Your song of mourning —
> So despised is God's own Son!
> God became the Man of Sorrows,
> Sentenced to die at Calvary.
> O ye mighty hosts of heaven,
> Mourn God's boundless agony!

The death sentence has been passed on Jesus, the Son of the living God! A verdict that makes heaven tremble, earth quake and hell break out in a rage. With this stroke hell achieved its greatest triumph — but at the same time suffered its greatest defeat. It lost everything. When Jesus accepted the death sentence in our stead, those who were condemned to death because of their sins were released, as we can see in the case of Barabbas, the first fruit of Jesus' death.

Up to this very day the thought of the Son of God being condemned to die allows man no peace. How was it possible that the Jews, that the crowds could demand Jesus' blood, His crucifixion? Surely many of those who shouted "Crucify him! Away with him!" had been healed by Him or had been among the thousands at the feeding of the multitudes, for instance. And so many knew Him, because He had done something for them personally, because they had witnessed His miracles and seen His glory, because they were indebted to Him for everything! How could it be that Jesus was nevertheless condemned to death?

Though we know that the Pharisees had bribed the rabble to shout "Crucify him!", more was involved. Quite apart from the Pharisees, the crowd itself was gripped by a sinister fury that made them frantically demand Jesus' death, shouting, "Crucify him!" It was the hour of darkness when the incomprehensible, the diabolical occurred. Crowds of people from Galilee, who owed Jesus their life and health, who had received love and blessings, help and comfort from Him in their physical and spiritual needs, now helped to put Him to death. Such an outcome was only possible, because in the previous years — in spite of all their esteem and affection for Jesus — they failed in one respect. They did not turn from their old, sinful ways. They did not wish to repent. This is what made Jesus lament over the cities in Galilee, where He had done most of His preaching and miracles. As a result of their sin of impenitence, they lapsed into the sin of ingratitude. Because they refused to make a break with their sins, they could not be filled with heartfelt gratitude and fervent love for Jesus.

Thus when Jesus came under such attack, they failed to bear witness to His good deeds and did not stand up for Him. Their impenitence and ingratitude opened the door for Satan to attack them in this crucial hour. And the terrible occurred: they had a part in causing the death sentence to be passed on Jesus. The very people whom Jesus should have been able to expect to stand up for Him out of gratitude, to intervene zealously for Him and His cause and prevent the death sentence and all the ensuing torment now assisted in bringing about His death.

And we? We are indebted to Jesus not only for helping us in some way or other, for healing or acts of kindness, but for our redemption, for eternal salvation and everlasting joy! Yet we act just like those Galileans if we do not turn away from our sins ever anew and make a radical break with them. Today when Jesus is crucified again, we do not speak out. We are not filled with gratitude and zeal to give an ardent testimony to Him, proclaiming who He is. If this were so, our love would be contagious, kindling many others with love for Jesus. Then the "death-of-God" theology could not gain so much ground within the Church. Then the dreadful blasphemy of Jesus could not sweep across the earth like wildfire. Then we would be prepared to testify all the more to that which Jesus has done for us when today the cry "Away with him!" is being raised throughout the nations and when even in churches He is no longer recognized as the Son of God and the Saviour of mankind.

If it is hard for the Jews to hear people say that they were responsible for Jesus' death, we can only stand at their side and admit that we too are responsible. For we belong to the great host of disciples that want to follow Jesus. If the disciples of long ago were at fault, because they did not combat the flames of hatred against Jesus that were kindled by the religious leaders of the time, we must confess that we too are responsible for Jesus' death sentence, because we take just as little trouble to beat down the flames of hatred against Jesus today for lack of love and gratitude. In comparison to the passionate hatred of Jesus' adversaries our love is often but a glimmering wick or a snuffed out candle. That explains why the death sentence could be pronounced over Jesus long ago and why the verdict that God is dead can pervade our countries today, why blasphemy and hatred have free rein and people once more raise the cry, "Away with him!"

all pray

Lord Jesus,

When we think of the burning hatred that You must suffer today as long ago when the death sentence was pronounced, we humble ourselves for all our lukewarmness, impenitence and ingratitude to You. As Your followers we have thus supported other people's rejection and even hatred of You today. Forgive us for standing by and watching while Satan's instruments today as of old are working zealously and attaining mighty victories. Forgive us that we are not on fire; forgive us that we do not spend ourselves in prayer and burn ourselves out in Your service.

O Holy Spirit, fill us now with an ardent love for our Lord Jesus Christ and the concerns of His kingdom.

Help us to be utterly self-forgetful, not heeding what may happen to us — even if we should suffer persecution. Help us to count it all as nothing in comparison to Your suffering today, Lord Jesus. Let our hearts and minds be centred on You. Fill us with love and gratitude to do everything in our power so that men may see You as the living and loving Lord and be inspired to give You their love. Help us in this way to stem the tide of blasphemy and hatred against You.

Our Lord Jesus, we thank You now and for evermore for permitting the death sentence to be pronounced upon You and for accepting it. Otherwise we would have been condemned to death, condemned to eternal punishment in hell. We long to bring You our gratitude by dedicating ourselves to You in ardent love and by offering our whole lives as a sacrifice.

Amen.

JESUS BEARS THE CROSS

all sing

O dearest Jesus mine,
Beneath the cross, my Saviour;
Your head is bowed in pain,
You came to earth to suffer.
To bear my sin and guilt
You go to Calvary.
Oh, I would praise You now,
My gracious Lord and King.

Jesus, my Life, my All,
How You now sway and falter!
Lord, who once through the heav'ns
Strode in majestic power,
Yours was the might of God,
Heavenly hosts adored,
Bowing to worship You —
But now You are so scorned.

Jesus, my dearest Lord,
Your cross is hard and heavy
And You are sore oppressed
By all the sins You're bearing.
They weigh upon the cross,
Pressing You to the ground.
O dearest Lamb of God,
How You are burdened down!

O Saviour, wounded sore!
With humble adoration
I give You praise and thanks
That You, for my salvation,

Patiently bore the cross,
Desired it fervently,
As though it were Your due,
In untold suffering.

melody EKG 66

My Saviour goes to suffer,
Belovèd Lamb of God.
O let me stay close by You
And share Your way, dear Lord.
Because of me You suffered
And for my sake You died.
Let me lament my sinning
And stay close by Your side.
O let me now go with You,
My dearest Lord and King;
Filled with contrition join You
In Your night of suffering.

*After Pilate left the seat of judgment, some of the soldiers followed him and took their positions in front of the palace for the procession. A small group accompanied the condemned Lord, who was led forward by the court servants. Several slaves passed through the gate carrying the cross, which they noisily threw down at Jesus' feet. As the cross lay on the ground before Him, Jesus fell on His knees and embraced it, softly uttering a loving prayer of thanksgiving to His heavenly Father that the redemption of mankind had begun.

The executioners pulled Jesus upright into a kneeling position and forced Him to take the heavy beam upon His right shoulder. This He did with great difficulty, clasping the cross with His right arm. He must have been assisted by unseen angels, for otherwise He could not have managed. Jesus was kneeling bowed down beneath the burden and while He prayed soldiers laid the horizontal bar of the crosses upon the necks of the two thieves.

A trumpet now resounded from Pilate's cavalry and Jesus was pulled to His feet. The whole burden of the cross was resting upon His shoulders. Then the procession began — on earth such a disgrace, in heaven such a triumph — as the King of kings went forth to redeem mankind. A detachment of several hundred soldiers followed on foot. At the head of the crucifixion procession was a trumpeter. At every street corner he blew his trumpet to announce the execution. A few steps behind the soldiers some of the rabble followed carrying ropes, nails, wedges and baskets with all sorts of tools. The more sturdy servants carried poles and ladders.

Then came our Lord and Saviour, stooping beneath the heavy burden of the cross, scourged, beaten, worn out. Since the Last Supper the previous night He had been without sleep, food or drink and continually subjected to murderous treatment. He was utterly exhausted from loss of blood, wound-fever, thirst and indescribable anguish of soul. He walked unsteadily, His bare feet covered with wounds. With His right hand He held the heavy burden on His right shoulder. With His left hand He often struggled to lift His loose garment as He walked with faltering steps. Four of the court servants tugged at Him with the ropes fastened to His belt of chains. His hands were wounded and swollen, because they had been so tightly bound. His face was covered with blood. His hair and beard were tangled and the strands were stuck together with blood. Under the pressure of the cross and the chains His heavy, woollen clothing clung to His wounded body and the wool stuck to the fresh wounds. Scorn and malice confronted Jesus on all sides. He was indescribably weak, immersed in suffering and yet overflowing with love. His lips moved in prayer. His pleading eyes were forgiving and sorrowful.

Jesus was led through a narrow, squalid lane, only a few feet wide. Here He had to suffer much. The court servants pressed closer to Him. People leaned out of the windows and peered through slits in the walls, laughing scornfully at Him. Then the street took a left turn, becoming somewhat wider and steeper. Rain water and filth would collect at this spot and here as at other places there was a raised stepping-stone. When Jesus reached this place with His heavy burden, He was unable to proceed any further. The executioners drove Him on mercilessly. Jesus stumbled over the projecting rock and fell to the ground, the cross falling down beside Him. Cursing and swearing, His tormentors pulled and kicked Him. The procession came to a halt and a tumult ensued. In vain Jesus stretched out His hand for someone to help Him.*

O lament! Jesus can no longer raise Himself. He who healed the sick and said, "Rise, take up your bed and go home!", yes, He who called out at the tomb of Lazarus, "Rise and come out!" now lies on the ground — powerless!

Let us pause and consider what immeasurable suffering our sin and guilt caused the Son of God here.

O lament! He who bore the dominion of the whole world upon His shoulders now breaks down beneath the burden of a cross.

O lament! He whom the princes of angels came to serve when He stretched out His arm now embraces the cross and can no longer carry it.

O lament! He who strode majestically through all the heavens, the King of glory, now bends low to the ground under the burden of the cross.

O lament! The Judge of the world, before whom the entire universe must bow one day, is subjected to such suffering. He now lies humiliated on the ground.

O lament what has happened! Man can no longer discern that Jesus is Lord and King. How faint He is now on the way of the cross! O Jesus, Creator of all worlds, great and omnipotent Lord, how weak You have become!

You humbled Yourself in the dust, desiring to become more lowly than man. We worship Your amazing love for us, which constrained You to humble Yourself so deeply.

all sing

    Lord, through Zion's streets so narrow,
    Stagg'ring 'neath the heavy cross,
    Deeply to that cross committed,
    Stopping not to rest or pause,
    Steadily You still go onward
    To Your goal, Mount Golgotha,
    Where You give Yourself as Victim
    On the cross they lifted there.

    Lord, for love of us, all bearing,
    Lord, for love of us, will die,
    Lord, for love of us, now hearing
    Words of scorn and blasphemy,
    Willing for our sake You carry
    Cross of shame to Calvary,
    For Your love saw not the anguish,
    But our chains and misery.

Jesus, Jesus, You have carried
All this poor world's guilty load.
Man of Sorrows, yet a Sovereign,
You have sin and Satan smote;
You for us have won the vict'ry
On the cross of Calvary.
We will praise You, Lord, for ever.
Lo! from sin You set us free.

melody WJ 69 or "Love
Divine, All Loves Excelling"

*With divine assistance Jesus raised His head once more. He was brutally dragged to His feet and the cross was laid again upon His shoulder. Now He had to hang His poor head, agonizingly pierced by the thorns, to one side in order to bear the heavy weight on His shoulder next to the wide crown of thorns. Afflicted with new and increased pain, He staggered on up the wide, rising street.

Mary, the mother of Jesus, pale and tearful, trembling and shaking, heard the uproar and the shouts of the approaching mob across the rooftops. She heard the sound of the trumpet and the announcement on the street corners that someone was being led off to be crucified. Thus she entered the street through which the procession had to pass. How the sound of the trumpet pierced her heart! The procession drew nearer. Soon it was only a few steps away. As the groups of executioners marched by with all their instruments of torture in impudent triumph, the mother of Jesus trembled and sobbed, wringing her hands. One of the executioners asked the passers-by, "Who is that woman weeping so piteously?" Someone replied, "It is the mother of the Galilean!"*

Meek and silent comes the Victim-
Sacrifice to Golgotha;
Here we sinners see the suff'ring
That we caused our God to bear.
Not one cry and no complaining
From His sacred lips we hear,
But His face so full of anguish,
Tortured limbs, wrung heart declares.

Yea, the Love of God is silent,
Patient bears the grief and pain.
This was planned for man's redemption;
Calv'ry did God foreordain.
Jesus walks the way of suff'ring,
Home He calls men lovingly,
Till fulfilled the world's salvation,
Sinners from all guilt set free.

Those for whom He took that pathway
See His pain but pass Him by;
Now as then it means but little
That for them He had to die.
So alone He bears their burdens.
Who of us sees there his own?
Who is moved by this, resolving
Every smallest sin to shun?

WJ 68

The procession then continued along a wide street passing through an arch in an ancient wall. Jesus staggered and stumbled once again, losing His grip on the cross. He fell to the ground, supporting Himself against a rock. A commotion ensued. The executioners could no longer bring Jesus to His feet and the Pharisees leading the procession said to the soldiers, "We shall never get him there alive. You had better find someone to carry his cross!" At that moment Simon of Cyrene, a gardener, was walking down the street. He could not escape owing to the crowd. When the soldiers saw from his clothes that he was a poor workman, they seized him and commanded him to help the Galilean to carry his cross. Simon resisted and showed great reluctance, for Jesus looked so dreadfully weak and disfigured. His garments were spattered with filth. But Jesus gave him such a piteous glance that Simon could not but assist Him. The executioners now bound the arm of the cross further back, fastening it with a sling to Simon's shoulder. He walked close behind Jesus, thus making it easier for Him to bear the weight. After the crown of thorns had been moved into a different position on Jesus' head, the sad procession was set into motion once more.

O Jesus, did You find no cross-bearer who would help You to carry Your cross? Where were all Your disciples? Where were the many people You had relieved of their burdens, so that they could walk about freely in the city? You set them free from bonds and chains, from evil spirits, from sickness and death. Where were they now? Oh, did no one come to bear Your cross with You?

all sing

> O Jesus, vainly did You yearn
> For one who would in pity turn;
> If but one soul had cast a thought,
> What comfort this to You had brought!
>
> Let me be now that soul I pray,
> Your pain relieve and soothe this day,
> And step by step with You keep pace.
> O Jesus, grant to me this grace.

I humbly will myself abase
If that will magnify Your grace.
I'll bear each burden patiently,
For it's the cross You give to me.

My cross I will praise constantly,
In it Your loving purpose see;
I will extol its power to bring
Much fruit of grace from suffering.

Humble and small I then shall be
If I but bear it patiently.
It opens wide the heav'nly gates,
Imprints on me Your loving traits.

You chose the cross for love of me;
So I would love it fervently.
I'll ever bear it after You;
May this, O Lord, now solace You.

melody WJ 71 or "Sun
of My Soul, Thou Saviour Dear"

choir

God seeks a soul who willingly
Will bear the cross in love,
Humbling himself as Jesus did.
O who will be this soul?

God seeks a soul who willingly
Will bear the cross in love,
Humbling himself as Jesus did.
Lord, let me be this soul!

When we think of how You bore the cross, O Lord
Jesus, we can only pray:

Along Your path of bitter sorrow You bowed so deeply beneath the burden of the cross. Now I would humble myself deeply before You and in shame confess my reluctance to bear the cross. Though innocent, You had to bear the burden of the cross, because I, a sinner, do not want to bear suffering, chastening, a cross — which I have deserved a hundred times over as the due reward of my sins. I ask Your forgiveness, my Lord Jesus, for the many times in my life when I have not borne my cross willingly, when I have sighed beneath it, when I have complained about burdens, rebelled against You in my heart and did not have You before my eyes, O Jesus, Cross-bearer of the world.

But remembering Your untold suffering while You carried the cross, I believe that You have redeemed me from my reluctance to bear the cross. In love and thanksgiving to You, who bore the cross for me to Calvary amid such torment, I will henceforth say, "I want to bear my cross, for it comes from Your hands. It is Your gift to me, O Lord; I will bear it gladly."

I want the cross. It brings only blessing. It is heavy, heavy-laden with gold.

I want the cross. It is precious and dear to me, for it transforms me into the image of God.

I want Your cross. I want to carry it after You, O Cross-bearer Jesus; I want to accompany You, my Lord.

And with all my heart I pray that You will help me to give thanks in pain and affliction when You count me worthy to bear suffering, to bear a cross for Your name's sake. Then let me live up to the words of Scripture, "Rejoice in so far as you share Christ's sufferings" and grant me a glimpse of the eternal glory that You have laid up for me above.

Let my suffering in the time of persecution grow insignificant when I consider the agony and torment You endured while carrying Your cross.

I thank You that I may suffer persecution united with You in the "fellowship of Your sufferings". And I thank You that at the same time I shall be immersed in Your love and experience the grace of Your presence — a foretaste of the heavenly bliss of eternal union.

Accept my committal. I want to enter the fellowship of Your sufferings, trusting in Your love, which is revealed above all to those who bear their cross.

Amen.

*Owing to the crowds of people that filled the streets, the procession came to a standstill. The executioners, furious at the delay, began to beat and pull Jesus. In the rough, bumpy lane there was a large puddle. And when Jesus stumbled again beneath the cross, He fell into the dirty puddle with such violence that Simon could scarcely hold the cross.

In a broken voice Jesus lamented, "Woe, woe, Jerusalem! How I have loved you! — like a hen that gathers her brood under her wings. And yet you cast Me so cruelly out of your gates!"

The Lord was very weak and deeply grieved.*

Does no one take Your part, O Lord,
On this Your bitter path of woe?
No! none consoles Your wounded heart
In its unfathomed sorrow.
By one and all You are forsaken now.

O that I could keep mourning,
Yes, mourning ceaselessly!
Though Thou art Love eternal,
So few bring love to Thee.

Thou long'st to have us near Thee,
But we go our own way.
We shun the path of suff'ring,
Avoid it day by day.

*The executioners struck and pushed Jesus and dragged Him out of the hole. When Jesus passed through the gate and came to the road leading to Calvary, He was met by a large group of weeping women. Seeing His appalling, wretched appearance, they raised their voices in loud lamentation and wept bitterly. According to the Jewish custom of showing sympathy, they held out cloths for Him to wipe the sweat from His face. Turning to them, Jesus said, "Daughters of Jerusalem, do not weep for me, but weep for yourselves and for your children. For behold, the days are coming when they will say, 'Blessed are the barren, and the wombs that never bore, and the breasts that never gave suck!' Then they will begin to say to the mountains, 'Fall on us'; and to the hills, 'Cover us!' "

He also said more, for instance, that their weeping would be rewarded and that they should now begin a new life.

The procession continued and Jesus was driven with the cross up the rugged, troublesome path from the city wall to Calvary. He was driven so violently that He stumbled and fell to the ground once more. Then Jesus was dragged up to Calvary, the place of execution, where He collapsed. Simon was driven away together with all the inquisitive rabble and the underlings who had followed the procession.*

Jesus had reached His goal. The Lamb of God, led to the slaughter, bearing the sacrificial altar on His own back, had completed His path.

> A cross will soon be lifted;
> God's Son will hang thereon.
> He bears our sins and burdens
> And we receive the crown.

> I thank You, Lord, You bore the heavy cross
> And with it all my sins so numerous.
>
> I thank You, Lord, You went to Calvary,
> That I can bear my cross now lovingly.
>
> I thank You, Lord, You fell beneath the cross;
> From fear of suff'ring You have ransomed us.
>
> I thank You, Lord. Because You went this way,
> Our souls may dwell above with You one day.
>
> O dearest Lord, You bore the cross for me.
> Your faithful "Simon" I now yearn to be.
>
> I thank You, Lord, thank You a thousandfold,
> O dearest Jesus, patient Lamb of God!

melody WJ 93

THE CRUCIFIXION

all sing

> O world, behold your life here,
> Upon the cross your Saviour
> Now in the throes of death.
> The mighty Prince of glory
> Bears willingly the mock'ry,
> The blows, insults and bitter scorn.
>
> O world, draw near and ponder
> This sight — His body covered
> With sweat and drops of blood.
> Because of untold suff'ring
> A thousand sighs are rising
> Within His heart immersed in pain.

cf. EKG 64

*After Simon of Cyrene was sent away and the executioners had finished their preparations for the crucifixion, they drove Jesus on with blows and taunts to the spot where they would nail Him to the cross. In the meantime, Jesus' mother, who in suffering love had been following the crucifixion procession at a distance, had reached the place of execution with her companions. The executioners, who had a type of wine that had been mixed with vermouth and myrrh, held a cup of this drink up to the lips of our Saviour, who stood in chains. He tasted it, but did not drink.

Now they tore off our Lord's cloak, which was draped over the upper part of His body. After removing the chains and His belt, they attempted to pull His white, woollen, seamless robe over His head. But since they were hindered by the wide crown of thorns, they tore the crown off His head, thus reopening the wounds. Then amid shameful words of derision they tore the handwoven robe off.

The Son of man stood there trembling, covered with blood and sores, streaks and stains, with dried up and bleeding wounds. He was wearing only a short woollen wrap for the upper part of His body and a loincloth for the lower part. The woollen fibres of the wrap were caught in the dried up wounds and stuck to the new deep wound, which had been inflicted by the burden of the cross where it had pressed into His shoulder. This wound caused Him immeasurable agony.

Mercilessly, they tore the wrap off His chest and His painful wounds were exposed to sight. His shoulder was torn to the bones. Now they ripped off the last remains of His clothing, the loincloth, from His hips. He stood there naked, cringing with shame. And as He threatened to collapse beneath their hands, they rolled up a stone and sat Him upon it, thrusting the crown of thorns down upon His head again.

But now, as the executioners pulled Him up in order to throw Him down upon the cross, there was indignant muttering, loud protest and mourning among all His friends about the shameful nakedness. At this Jesus was handed a cloth, which He gratefully accepted and wrapped about His body.*

Jesus, the Fairest, disfigured, disgraced!
Jesus, the Highest, dishonoured, abased!
Jesus, God's Son — rejected,
Rejected by sinners,
By us, His own children,
Rejected, disgraced in the eyes of the world!
Your suff'ring, O Jesus, expresses Your love.
O Lord, hear our plea. Forgive us our sins!

JESUS IS NAILED TO THE CROSS

*Now the executioners came to stretch Jesus out upon the cross. Jesus, a sight to arouse pity, sat down on it by Himself. Then they pushed Him down on His back, pulled His right arm to the nail hole in the right arm of the cross and bound it there with ropes. One of the executioners knelt down upon His holy chest, while another held open His hand, which tried to close. And a third placed a long, thick nail, which was filed to a point, into His right hand, which had blessed so many. The nails were so long that when they were held in a fist, they stuck out above and below. And now as the nail was furiously rammed into His hand with an iron hammer, His blood spurted on to the arms of the executioners.

After the right hand of our Lord had been nailed to the cross, the crucifiers discovered that His left hand, which was also tied on to the cross, did not reach the hole that they had bored. The tips of His fingers were quite a distance from the hole. Accordingly, they bound ropes on to His left hand and tugged vigorously — bracing themselves with their feet up against the cross — until His hand reached the place for the nail. The crucifiers then knelt down upon Jesus' arm and chest. They fastened His arm with a rope and brutally drove the second nail through the left hand of our Lord.*

Let us pray together:

all pray

O that You had to endure such torment because of us! Lord Jesus, forgive us! O innocent Lord, because of our sin You suffered nails to be driven through Your hands and feet in such inhuman cruelty! Forgive us! Have mercy upon us who have caused You such abysmal torment and agony with our sin and who time and again do not take sin seriously, although we know what inhuman torture it cost You. We entreat You, may this dreadful event, Your being nailed to the cross, strike our heart like the blow of a hammer. May we respond to Your agonizing suffering by hating sin and by desiring in love and gratitude to do only that which would bring joy to Your heart, no matter what it may cost us.

Help us to accept the Father's chastening blows wholeheartedly, for we have deserved them. We no longer want to grieve You with our rebellion against such blows, for You endured the cruel blows during the nailing, which caused You such pain and inflicted bleeding wounds.

Our Lord Jesus, as sinners, we surrender ourselves to bear wounds in body, soul and spirit, including those inflicted upon us by people who hurt our feelings and insult us. As we remember the dreadful wounds that the nails inflicted upon You, let us consider it an honour when cruel blows, torment and derision inflict many wounds upon us — especially in the time of persecution — for then You take us into the fellowship of Your sufferings.

Let us never forget that our sins have covered You, our Lord and God, with wounds.

Amen.

choir

> Who can understand it, O dearest Lord,
> That You, God's own Son, must bear wounds and
>   scorn!
> Who can understand what man dares to do!
> O Lamb, sorely wounded, I worship You.

Your heart is pure love — mild, yet ardent too;
The Father's own beauty shines forth from You!
We mourn and bewail what we dared to do:
Inflicting cruel wounds, we crucified You.

choir

For ever and ever, O Lamb divine,
The marks of Your wounds through the universe
  shine.
And through all the heavens one song resounds —
The song of Your bride, adoring Your wounds.

The Mother Mary and His devoted followers, who were witnesses of this torment, felt all the agony with Jesus.

O that we may be fully absorbed with Jesus' bitter suffering and torment! May our prayer be that we bear in our hearts Jesus' agony, His great suffering long ago and today when so many wounds are inflicted upon Him, when His heart is pierced anew and cruel words are flung at Him. May God grant us the high privilege of partaking of Jesus' sufferings today.

Jesus is longing for people who will suffer with Him in His agony. What was the sole comfort Jesus received in His Passion? The presence of those who shared His suffering — His mother, Mary Magdalene and John beneath the cross. Jesus yearns for such souls. O let us ask for the grace to bear His agony in our hearts, that everything else may grow unimportant to us and that we may be completely drawn into His suffering.

all sing

May Thy sore wounds be imprinted
Deep within my heart, O Lord.

May I ever think upon them
And forget them nevermore.
Thou my highest Good indeed,
My heart findeth rest in Thee!
Let me at Thy feet, my Saviour,
Taste Thy boundless love and favour.

cf. *Altes bayrisches Gesangbuch* 122

But while the mother of Jesus bore all the agony with Him, the Pharisees sneered and made insults, looking in her direction. Mary Magdalene, who stood next to her, was beside herself with grief.

Oh, if only we bore in our hearts some of this sorrow for Jesus! It will be imparted to us in the measure that we come to see our sin and weep over it. And in the same measure we shall weep over that which our sin inflicts upon Jesus. Then we shall hate sin with such vehemence that other souls will also begin to loathe sin and yearn to be set free.

After our Saviour's arms had been forcibly stretched to meet the holes, which had been bored too far apart, His body was pulled upward and His knees were drawn up. The executioners fell upon Him and bound down His knees with ropes. But His feet were far above the foot block due to the placing of the holes. The executioners began to curse and sneer. Some said new holes should be bored for the arms, because it was too much trouble to move the foot block higher. Others taunted Him, saying that He didn't want to stretch, but that they would help Him. They tied ropes on to His right leg, pulled it down to the block with dreadful violence and fastened it tight with a rope. The strain on the body was so great that Jesus uttered loud cries of lamentation, "O God! O God!" They had also bound His chest and arms to prevent His hands from tearing away from the nails. The suffering was immeasurable.

choir

> Come, O come in hosts unnumbered,
> Men, and angels round the throne.
> Come, surround the Lord with weeping.
> He, God's pure and holy Son,
> For our sake and our transgressions
> Now is nailed upon the cross.
> Oh, His torment and His suff'ring
> Tell of His great love for us!

*The nailing of Jesus' feet to the cross exceeded all previous torment. The cruel hammer blows resounded together with the laments of our Saviour. The furious, taunting voices about Him were muffled. Jesus uttered pure cries of pain as He prayed passages from the Psalms and the prophets whose prophecies He was now fulfilling. From the very beginning of His Passion to the moment of His death He was continually in such prayer.

When they began to nail Him to the cross, the leader of the Roman guard had the title that Pilate had written nailed on a block at the head of the cross. The Pharisees were annoyed, because the Romans laughed loudly at the title, "King of the Jews". Some of the Pharisees then rode back down into the city to ask Pilate for a different inscription.*

THE CROSS IS ERECTED

*After our Lord was nailed to the cross, His tormentors pulled the cross up with ropes and edged it towards the hole. Then they tilted the upper end a little way forward. It was a frightening sight when amidst the jeering shouts of the executioners and the Pharisees and the crowd, which could now see Him, the cross swayed through the air.

Sympathizing and mourning voices also rose about Him. His mother and Mary Magdalene, the disciple and all those of God-fearing heart broke out in a great lamentation as they greeted the eternal Word, manifest in the flesh, raised upon the cross. And all the hands of those who loved Him were lifted anxiously as if they wanted to help, now that the cross was raised by the hands of furious sinners — the cross on which the Most Holy of all, the Bridegroom of souls, was nailed alive.

Then the executioners pushed the cross into a vertical position and with its whole weight it was violently rammed into the hole with a shuddering thud. According to the position of the sun, it may have been about 12 noon as they erected the cross.

The sound of many trumpets could now be heard from the Temple, announcing that the slaughtering of the paschal lamb had begun. The solemn notes of the trumpets sounded out above the jeering shouts and the cries of lamentation for the true Lamb of God that was being slain. Many a hard heart was stirred and remembered the words of John the Baptist, "Behold, the Lamb of God, who takes away the sin of the world!" And after the cross had been placed in the hole with a loud thud, even the sneers were interrupted for a few minutes by an astonished silence. A strange feeling came over everyone present. Even hell felt the thrust of the sinking cross with terror and lashed out once more in rebellion with taunts and curses.

But the souls in the kingdom of the dead were seized

with deep yearning and joy. They heard the thrust with hope and expectation. It sounded to them like the knocking of the approaching Victor on the gates of redemption. Like a second tree of life in paradise the holy cross was now erected in the middle of the world and from Jesus' wounds there flowed streams of His holy blood upon the earth.*

choir

> A cross is raised!
> Upon it — God's own Son!
> O cross of grace so glorious,
> Shining through all the universe,
> Bearing the tidings that we are loved,
> That God the Father forgives us, forgives!
>
> A cross is raised!
> Upon it — God's own Son!
> He bore our sins to Calvary.
> We are redeemed, we are redeemed,
> To bear God's image evermore!

O holy cross, now towering up in the middle of the earth, none can fail to see you. As an eternal symbol of victory, you stand there bearing the holy burden, the innocent Son of God and man, who was raised upon the cross, so that all who believe in Him should not perish.

O holy cross, now you stand erected as the tree of life, from which streams of life, Jesus' holy blood, flow unceasingly, granting salvation to all who come to drink and be filled, to be cleansed of all sins.

Jesus is now wedded to the cross, the symbol of salvation, the symbol of redemption, the symbol of victory, the symbol of all the wondrous power of God.

We lift up our voices in praise. In the cross there is power and might, for as the cross was rammed into the earth, hell was shaken. Towering up to heaven, the cross points the way to the throne of grace for those who throw themselves down at its foot, weeping over their sins. And just as its arms stretch in all directions, Jesus' outstretched arms bring lost children from all the ends of the earth home to the Father.

O cross, now standing before us in this holiest of hours, in you we find salvation. You stand there majestically, for the One who was crucified upon you has overcome in all His suffering — the Lamb that was led to the slaughter, the Lamb that vanquished the power of hell.

O praise and worship, for the hour of salvation and redemption has come! Fall down in adoration! From now on no one need perish who believes in the crucified Lord. Come and worship, for upon this cross hangs the Son of God. Behold this cross, where now His blood streams down. In spirit drink in His blood, that you may be healed.

Because the place where the cross was standing protruded above the ground, Jesus' friends could embrace His feet and kiss them when the foot of the cross was set into the hole.

Now Jesus hangs upon the cross. All who are standing round can see Him. He is raised above this earth.

Oh, if only everyone would want to see Him, if only all eyes would want to look upon the dearest Lamb of God, if only all would embrace His feet! If only all would show Him their love now for the love that He did not receive along His bitter path of shame and suffering to Calvary!

Now He hangs upon the cross and from this moment on people are filled with love and adoration for Him.

From this moment on Jesus is looked upon in tender love, whereas previously people had turned their eyes away from Him, as He was being led through the crowds, shamefully disfigured. This moment signifies the beginning of something wonderful: one look at the cross upon which Jesus hangs changes men's hearts and brings them to contrition and repentance. One look at the cross melts human hearts and kindles them with love. Heavy-laden consciences are unburdened and fetters are broken. Those who were in despair over their sins are filled with joy. As the Lamb of God hung dying upon the cross, the hour of His victory began.

Now the Father is waiting for people everywhere to hasten to the cross, to adore the Lamb of God, and to receive salvation from His wounds. Let us come to Him in this hour to worship and praise Him.

all sing

> All hail to You, O Jesus,
> Now nailed upon the tree.
> O holy Lord in torment,
> O gentle, suff'ring King!
> All hail to You, O Jesus, O Jesus!
>
> All hail, O Lamb most holy,
> Tormented on the cross.
> All hail, O Love eternal,
> Wed to the cross for us.
> All hail to You, O Jesus, O Jesus!
>
> All hail to You, O Jesus;
> Your hands and feet are nailed.
> Your love makes expiation
> For all our sin and guilt.
> All hail to You, O Jesus, O Jesus!

All hail to You, Lord Jesus,
In all Your agony.
You ransomed us, Your children;
From sin You set us free.
All hail to You, O Jesus, O Jesus!

We hail Your heart, O Jesus,
In all its pain and grief.
Our host of sins so grievous
Has caused Your agony.
All hail to You, O Jesus, O Jesus!

May You be blessed for ever
By all for whom You died,
Our loving thanks we bring You,
Lord Jesus, crucified!
All hail to You, O Jesus, O Jesus!

melody WJ 76

Up to this moment Jesus was despised and ridiculed, the butt of scorn. But the moment that He hung upon the cross, He was placed in a different light. Now everything that was associated with Jesus was suddenly highly valued, and the soldiers gambled for His robe. Jesus' sacrifice was almost completed. And whenever a sacrifice has been completed, the fruit begins to show — though not until then! It was not during Jesus' way of suffering, but rather as He hung upon the cross that the fruit of His suffering emerged. It was then that a centurion broke down and repented and many beat their breasts. It was then that wonders and signs took place. But not until then!

Along Jesus' path to the cross, even the heavenly world did not seem to be involved. Jesus was supposed to appear like a criminal, rejected by the world, forsaken by God and man, despised, delivered up to His adversaries and the arch-enemy himself. Neither God nor man intervened on His behalf any more. In the sight of the whole world He was the guilty one. Not until the sacrifice had been completed, did God — as it were — emerge from His silence, which seemed to testify against the Son. Now God began to justify the innocence of the Son in the sight of all the world by letting His creation declare what had happened here. He caused the sun to grow dark and opened the graves. With that God pronounced His yea and amen, testifying that Jesus was crucified as the innocent Lamb of God.

When we, who are sinners, have to walk a path of suffering in our personal lives, such spiritual laws apply to us too. This truth should help us in hard times to wait steadfastly for the hour of divine intervention and to believe that after we have walked a path of suffering to the end, the glory of God will be manifest and God will bring forth the fruit. However, as we can see in Jesus' Passion, this cannot come to pass until the path of suffering has been completed.

But even though Jesus' sacrifice on the cross was almost completed, He still had to suffer the bitter death.

*After the cross was violently lowered into the hole, Jesus' head, laden with the crown of thorns, was cruelly jolted and streams of blood flowed down. Streams of His holy blood also flowed from His hands and feet. The executioners now climbed up the ladders they had set up and removed the ropes from the holy body with which they had bound Him to the cross to prevent Him from tearing loose from the nails when the cross was erected. Owing to the change from a horizontal to a vertical position and the loosening of the ropes, His blood began to circulate more quickly and He could feel afresh the excruciating pain. Jesus lowered His head

144

upon His chest and hung there unconscious for several minutes as though dead.

A moment of silence reigned. The trumpet calls from the Temple died away. All those present were utterly exhausted by fury or grief. And Jesus, the Salvation of the world, faint from His pains, hung motionless upon the cross. His head, laden with the dreadful crown of thorns, was sunk upon His chest. Even later, due to the size of the crown, He could only lift His head with immeasurable agony. His chest was stretched, His shoulders looked gaunt and were terribly strained. His elbows and wrists seemed to be pulled out of their sockets. Blood streamed down His arms from the wounds in His hands that had been torn open so wide. His hips and legs too seemed to be dreadfully wrenched out of their sockets. His limbs were extended so cruelly, the muscles so strained and His lacerated skin so taut that all His bones could be counted. Blood also trickled down the cross beneath the terrible nail that had bored through His holy feet — and His sacred body was entirely covered with sores and bruises, red weals and bleeding wounds. Later the body of Jesus grew increasingly pale, as though it had been drained of all its blood.

Yet in spite of such terrible disfigurement the body of our Lord upon the cross bore the mark of ineffable majesty. Indeed, the Son of God, eternal Love, who entered time and gave Himself as a sacrifice, was pure and holy — beautiful to behold — although His body, laden with the sins of mankind, was bruised and battered. The Lamb of God was being slain.*

> O Life divine, we see Thee suff'ring
> Upon the cross of Calvary.
> Thou sacrificed Thyself completely
> To waken in us love for Thee.

O Lord, Thy body is disfigured,
Exposed and beaten, full of wounds,
And so we see Thee, dearest Saviour —
O wondrous love that knows no bounds!

O Lord, with all our love and fervour
We praise Thee in humility
And yearn to bring Thee thanks for ever
For Thine unfathomed agony.

*After the thieves had been crucified, the executioners gathered all their tools together; then cursing and taunting Jesus, they went their way. The Pharisees that were still present also insulted Him with many shameful words and departed. The numerous Roman soldiers and their leaders left the place of execution, because they were relieved by a new group of soldiers with their centurion.

Another group of Pharisees, Sadducees, scribes and a few elders arrived together with those who had gone in vain to ask Pilate for a new inscription for the cross. Pilate would not even admit them and this embittered them all the more.

The blasphemers walked round the cross, and when they passed in front of Jesus, they shook their heads disparagingly at Him and called out, "Shame on you, you liar! How can you destroy the Temple and build it up again in three days?" "He always wanted to help others, but he can't help himself!" "If you are the Son of God, come down from the cross!" "If he is the King of Israel, let him come down and then we'll believe!" "He trusted in God; so let God help him now!" The soldiers reviled Him too and shouted, "If you are the King of the Jews, then help yourself now!"*

Up to the very minute of His death Jesus was perse-cuted with scorn, ridicule and disgrace; thus we can see that it is the favourite weapon of the devil and the kingdom of hell. It is one of the most underhanded meth-ods of attack, for it is more subtle than outright attack, and less obvious in its effects. But it inflicts deep wounds upon the souls of others. Jesus had to atone for this sin by suffering derision in full. He drank the cup of scorn and blasphemy to the dregs.

O Lord, when we contemplate this suffering of Yours, we beg forgiveness for every time we have committed this sin.

*The scoffing went on. Jesus, however, raised His head a little and said, "Father, forgive them; for they know not what they do!" and He continued to pray quietly. The wicked thief cried out in derision, "If you are Christ, save yourself and save us!" But the thief on the right was deeply moved as Jesus prayed for His enemies, and through Jesus' prayer he was suddenly spiritually enlightened. He said to the other thief, "Don't you fear God when you are suffering the same sentence? We deserve this torment; we are receiving the due reward of our deeds. But this man has done no wrong!" He was inwardly convicted and confessed his sins, growing more and more penitent. In humble hope he lifted his head towards Jesus and said, "Lord, if You condemn me, it would be only just, but have mercy upon me! — Lord, remember me when You come into Your kingdom!" And Jesus not only said to him, "Yes, I shall remember you," but promised, "Today you will be with Me in paradise; today you will taste the joy of paradise!" *

"Today," Jesus says, "this very day!" These words upon the cross give a glimpse of the coming victory. Today Jesus' suffering will be ended; today He will enter paradise in triumph. Only a short while and He will have overcome.

Let us hear Jesus today when He speaks so graciously to us too, saying that if we repent *today*, we shall receive forgiveness *today*, and then the gates of paradise will be opened to us *today!*

At last our Lord Jesus can depart from this dreadful earth, this lair of murderers, where He was blasphemed, tortured and killed. At last He can return to the Father's house, His true home, and resume His eternal glory. And with Him He brings souls like the thief — wretched but pardoned sinners, beautifully clad in His righteousness.

O Jesus, how can we ever express our gratitude? In all eternity we shall not be able to thank You enough!

And now as Jesus hung upon the cross in inhuman torment, one sign after another occurred to vindicate Him and thus proclaim His victory.

At about the sixth hour the sky suddenly became very dark and the stars glowed a reddish hue. The solar disc was visibly darkened. Only a pale gleam remained. A profound fear came over man and beast. Animals roared and charged away. Birds sought hiding places and fell down in flocks upon the hills round Calvary. It was possible to grasp them with the hand.

Now it is no longer Jesus who is made to be afraid. Now fear comes upon those who were torturing Him to death. Now the tide begins to turn. The hour of recompense is dawning.

The hour of divine recompense will come very soon in our age too. Today Jesus is suffering anew the hour of Gethsemane and of the crucifixion — this time on a world-wide scale — when the nations are crucifying Him again by their abominations and diabolical sins, which are mounting up to heaven. Once again the "hour of darkness" is striking, but this time darkness is covering

148

all the nations. They all dare to attack God, to heap terrible blasphemy upon Jesus. Today once more the shout is being raised throughout the world, "Away with Jesus!" The shout "Crucify!" will soon be hurled at His disciples too, and many will be made to suffer death. But they will be able to endure it if they fix their gaze upon the Lamb of God that was crucified for them. And when they have laid down their lives as a sacrifice, the tide will turn once more. God will once more emerge from His silence; miracles will occur and judgment will descend, and all the blasphemers and offenders will be destroyed.

In this hour of God's judgment, when His holy wrath descends upon the earth, the scoffers will fall silent — just as the jeering of the Pharisees was finally silenced as they witnessed the shattering events during the hour of the crucifixion.

May the heavenly Father receive love and gratitude for having given these signs to justify His Son and having taken Jesus' part again in the sight of all. Now He spoke on Jesus' behalf through the mighty natural phenomena. Thanks be to the Father! In the hour of the Son's death, He intervened on His behalf, restoring the honour of His Son and revealing that our Lord Jesus Christ, condemned and crucified like a criminal, was the pure and innocent Son of God.

*The mother of Jesus, Mary Magdalene, Mary the wife of Clopas, and John stood beneath the cross with their eyes fixed on the Lord. In her heart, the Mother Mary was fervently entreating Him to let her die with Him. Then Jesus looked at His mother earnestly and compassionately; and turning His eyes to John, He said to her, "Woman, behold, this is your son!" To John He said, "Behold, this is your mother!" And reverently, like a devoted son, John embraced the mother of Jesus, who

149

had now also become his mother, beneath the cross of the dying Saviour.

In the city there was general panic and confusion. Fog and darkness enwrapped the streets. People groped about confused. Many huddled in corners, covering their heads. Others stood on the roofs and lamented as they looked up at the sky. Pilate visited Herod and in great consternation they surveyed the sky from the same terrace where Herod had watched Jesus being mocked that morning. They were highly alarmed and strode vigorously back and forth surrounded by guards.

On Calvary the darkness made a frightening impression. At first the attention of all had been diverted from the slowly darkening sky by the many other impressions — the terrible raging and the torture, the screaming and cursing as the cross was erected, the roaring of the two thieves, the Pharisees' sneering and pacing to and fro, the changing of the guard, and the noisy departure of the drunken executioners. Then followed the confession of the repentant thief.

But now the darkness increased. The spectators became more pensive. Most of them gazed up at the sky. Many consciences were stirred. Some of the onlookers turned their eyes to the cross in contrition. Falling down on their knees, they asked forgiveness of Jesus, and Jesus looked upon them in His agony. Those who were of the same mind gradually drew together. The Pharisees, who were secretly afraid, still tried to explain things naturally, but their speeches grew more and more subdued, and finally they fell almost completely silent. Now and then they made a contemptuous remark, but it sounded very contrived. The orb of the sun turned an ashy grey. The stars came out in a reddish colour. The donkeys of the mounted Pharisees pressed close together and hung their heads. Vapour and fog enveloped everything. All was silent round the cross. The crowds had withdrawn. Many fled into the city. The crucified Saviour was utterly forsaken. But in His infinite suffering He lovingly interceded for His enemies. He had fully turned to His heavenly Father and once more prayed the words of the Psalms that were now being fulfilled in Him.

The darkness increased even more. Fear overcame the conscience-stricken people and a stifling silence lay upon them all while Jesus hung utterly forsaken and unconsoled on the cross.*

As God the Father now began to take Jesus' part openly and to judge the world through these natural catastrophes, Jesus still had to drink the last remains of the cup. He had to drink the most bitter part at the very moment when we would think that Jesus, full of gratitude, could sense, "The Father is present, the Father is speaking on My behalf, testifying that I am His Son, establishing My innocence on the cross!" No, while this is taking place, the Son is unable to perceive it. In His heart He now feels utterly forsaken by God. This was the last measure of affliction that Jesus had to endure.

*Jesus suffered everything that a tormented and crushed person suffers when he is utterly forsaken by God and deprived of all human and divine comfort. The grief is inexpressible when faith, hope and love find no response, no fulfilment, no light, but are laid bare and made void as they languish alone in the desert of trials with immeasurable agony. In this suffering Jesus' amazing love won for us the strength to be victorious in the greatest misery, when we are forsaken, when all human ties and relationships on earth have come to an end. Having been immersed in the bitter depths of the agony of being forsaken by God and man on the cross,

Jesus is able to reach down and save us from being forsaken in death. May we never forget that the agony of being forsaken was more bitter for Jesus than it could have ever been for a human being, because He was actually one with the Father, being wholly God and wholly man. As God-man He had to suffer the state of a God-forsaken humanity to the full.*

all pray

Dear Lord Jesus, our Lord and Saviour,

As sinful men not one of us can have even an inkling of the suffering You underwent as the Son of the Father when You were forsaken. Though one with the Father, You seemed to be repelled by Him — and this You endured because of our sin. You took upon Yourself our sins and thus became separated from the Father and from heaven.

Dearest Lord Jesus, our sin lay upon You; our iniquities covered You as the countless sores and wounds on Your tormented body declare.

Lord Jesus, not only were You made one with suffering, You were made sin for us and therefore You were forsaken by God. You were totally separated from God, Your Father, although You are God.

O Lord Jesus, what have we inflicted upon You! How appalling sin is! O Holy Spirit, give us an unequalled hatred of sin, for sin creates hell and Jesus had to pay for sin with such agonizing pain.

Amen.

*At about three o'clock Jesus, in His suffering, called out with a loud voice, expressing His utter forsakenness, "'Eli, Eli, lama sabachthani?', that is, 'My God, my God, why hast thou forsaken me?'"

Soon after three it became light. The sun had no radiance; it was red and surrounded by a haze. Little by little the rays returned, although the sky was still overcast.

The body of the Lord on the cross looked pale, as though it had been completely drained of blood. His tongue was parched as He spoke, "I thirst!"

While Jesus hung there so wretched and faint, a soldier fastened a sponge dipped in vinegar to a staff and held it up to Jesus.

As the end drew near, our Lord wrestled with death and a cold sweat covered His limbs. The disciple John stood at the cross. Mary Magdalene, distraught with grief, leaned against the back of the cross. The Mother Mary, standing between Jesus' and the good thief's cross, supported by Mary the wife of Clopas and Salome, looked up at her dying Son. Then Jesus spoke, "It is finished!" He raised His head and called out with a loud voice, "Father, into thy hands I commit my spirit!" It was a loud, heart-moving cry, piercing heaven and earth. Then He sank His head and yielded up His spirit.*

Let us be silent for a few minutes.

choir
  Behold the Lamb of God! It is finished!

*With the earthquake at Jesus' death, when the rock of Calvary was split, many things in the world fell and collapsed — especially in the Holy Land and in Jerusalem — as a result of the triumphant victory of the Lamb. Now the fruit became visible. Now the power of His death was demonstrated. At the rumbling of the

153

earth tremor and the sound of the curtain in the Temple being torn, fear and consternation befell all who were gathered in the Temple for the slaughtering of the paschal lamb — thousands of people.

With the appearing of the dead all the proceedings in the Temple came to a standstill. The sacrifice was interrupted, as though the Temple had been defiled. The festival was dissolved. For the true Paschal Lamb had come and been slain, and the world was redeemed.*

all pray

Our Lord Jesus,

We worship You. Now it is finished! You have accomplished the redemption of all mankind, having made full atonement for sin. Now whoever believes in You will not perish. Your heart, O Lord Jesus Christ, was broken with grief and now salvation flows from Your wounded side to all who come and drink from You, the Source of life.

We worship You, dear Lord Jesus, for You bowed Your head and called out, "It is finished!"

Praise and glory be to You, Lord Jesus Christ, for You abolished death. Although You died, You descended into the kingdom of the dead as the Lord of life! You have vanquished sin and Satan. Their power is broken! You are Victor over every power that can be named!

Praise be to You, Lord Jesus, O dying Love! Victorious in death, You brought forth new life in defeat and won eternal salvation.

Praise be to You, O Lamb of God, who bore the sins of the world on the cursed tree, making it a tree of blessing for all generations in the hour of Your death. We worship You, almighty, eternal Son of God, O Lamb that was slain! Now the dreadful agony and torment of the slaughter is over. The sacrifice is completed. You have overcome! The way of the cross and the sufferings of the crucifixion have come to an end. O Lord Jesus Christ, You have triumphed. You have broken the power of death! Eternal salvation has been wrought for all mankind!

Amen.

Glory, glory, glory to the Lamb,
Henceforth and for evermore.   Amen.

choir

O come, adore,
O come, adore!
The Lamb hath died to ransom us.

Lord, we adore,
Lord, we adore!
Salvation Thou hast wrought for us.

SUGGESTIONS FOR HOLDING
THE PASSION SERVICE

At Canaan we have the custom of preparing ourselves beforehand for the Passion Service. On Maundy Thursday each one searches his heart once more before God to see whether he is reconciled with everyone or whether he still should go to someone to ask forgiveness in the spirit of humility that Jesus showed at the footwashing (John 13). For "by this all men will know that you are my disciples, if you have love for one another". And as we think of the times when we have especially sinned against love in the past year, Maundy Thursday is a challenge to us to express our contrition and repentance once more.

During the Passion Service it has proved to be helpful if every participant has the following: a Bible, a copy of this book, a book for personal notes, a hymnal and a copy of *Well-spring of Joy* as well as *Glory Be to God*.

The tape recording of this service may be stopped from time to time for the participants to give their response individually or as a group, to bring Jesus Christ their thanksgiving and praise, to write down prayers of renunciation, make new acts of dedication and to express their love for Him in song.

Books by M. Basilea Schlink, supplementing the topic of this book

BEHOLD HIS LOVE 144 pp.

Nothing can bring us closer to Jesus than meditating upon His Passion, for in doing so we search the depths of His heart. This book will help us to find a warm, vital relationship with our Saviour when we behold His amazing love which compelled Him to choose suffering and death for our sakes.

MY ALL FOR HIM 160 pp.

"Here is described first-hand, vital, all-demanding discipleship, but not as an ideal possible only to the few — for it depends not upon our abilities but upon our Lord's love burning in our hearts."

IN OUR MIDST — JESUS LOVES AND SUFFERS TODAY 32 pp.

Jesus still lives and suffers today. The cross is not just a past event of history; we cause Him fresh pain every time we neglect God's Commandments; we grieve Him when we refuse to repent. We fail to recognize Jesus in our midst, because we do not love Him. The message of this booklet is a plea that we should turn to Him for forgiveness and so enter into the personal relationship of love with Him for which we were created.

WELL-SPRING OF JOY, 272 songs of the Sisters of Mary for singing or praying

"The songs of Mother Basilea spring from a heart so full of love for Jesus, so tuned to the voice of the Holy Spirit, that through them the deep things of God are revealed, expressed in words and music beautifully combined. Each song becomes a prayer whereby I can reach out to His heart of love."

THE HOLY LAND TODAY   368 pp.
Revised edition 1975

The Holy Land comes to life — a guidebook with a difference! Through the prayers and devotional passages the reader is confronted with the challenge of the holy places and the memorable events associated with the life and sufferings of the Lord Jesus. A treasure indeed! Pilgrims will find it an indispensable companion as they follow in the footsteps of Jesus. Others, unable to make a pilgrimage, will turn to this book again and again as they too, in spirit, relive those scenes of long ago. A book for all who seek a deeper and more personal relationship to Jesus.   A reader, Jerusalem.